WESTMINSTER WOMEN

WESTMINSTER WOMEN

LINDA MCDOUGALL

V

VINTAGE

Published by Vintage 1998

2 4 6 8 10 9 7 5 3 1

First published in Great Britain by
Vintage

Vintage
Random House, 20 Vauxhall Bridge Road, London SW1V 2SA

Random House Australia (Pty) Limited
20 Alfred Street, Milsons Point, Sydney
New South Wales 2061, Australia

Random House New Zealand Limited
18 Poland Road, Glenfield,
Auckland 10, New Zealand

Random House South Africa (Pty) Limited
Endulini, 5A Jubilee Road, Parktown 2193, South Africa

Random House UK Limited Reg. No. 954009

A CIP catalogue record for this book
is available from the British Library

ISBN 0 09 927405 1

Papers used by Random House UK Ltd are natural, recyclable
products made from wood grown in sustainable forests. The
manufacturing processes conform to the environmental
regulations of the country of origin

Typeset by SX Composing DTP, Rayleigh, Essex
Printed and bound in Great Britain by
Cox & Wyman Ltd, Reading, Berkshire

CONTENTS

ACKNOWLEDGEMENTS

THIS BOOK COULD not have been written without my husband Austin Mitchell. His career as the MP for Grimsby has allowed me twenty years' access to Parliament as a Westminster wife. His wit and good humour when faced with my constant criticisms of Westminster men, and his pride and joy in his three independent and successful daughters makes him more of a feminist than most.

My son, Jonathan Mitchell has also been critical to this venture. He has been by my side as a film maker and friend through six months nervously creeping round the corridors of Westminster trying to avoid the eye of authority, and spent endless wet Saturdays in dreary town halls waiting for the MP to finish her busines.

Marion Bowman commissioned the documentaries which started this off. Phil Craig, Lucy Stylianou, Eve Laidlaw, Rosey Igglesden and Susie Calderan have all given me strong support at work.

Meg Russell, the Labour Party's women's officer helped a lot and Tim Grewall, Austin's research assistant at the House of Commons has been generous with his time and advice and trips to the library.

Philip Wright and his colleagues in the Sergeant-at-Arms' Office at Westminster have helped us to rattle the barricades, if not to dismantle them.

Maggie Pearlstine and Matthew Baylis have been marvellous supporters for a nervous new author and I owe a lot to them.

Most of my thanks is reserved for the poet and novelist Kate Bingham who has been by my side since this project was commissioned, researching and writing about Westminster Women. Not only has she been my partner in the writing of the book, she's turned her hand to all the technical aspects of film production required these days when projects are made by small independent production companies. I have made a friend for life and I owe her a great debt.

INTRODUCTION: ONE MAY MORNING

IN THE PAVILION in Cleethorpes, people were packed tighter than onions in a pickle jar. Arms around each other in the cold early morning of 2 May 1997 they spilled into the road, celebrating the unique experience of a Labour victory. Most of them were young and could not remember life before the Tories.

My husband Austin and I fought our way through the room to the bar, where a huge square sponge cake sat on a silver board. 'Congratulations Austin', read the icing writing, 'Twenty years as MP for Grimsby'. A small grey-haired group of survivors struggled over to join us. Twenty years before we had been the proud and exhausted Party workers when Austin won the Grimsby by-election by 520 votes – a night of pure joy that will remain in my memory for ever.

This was the fifth general election since that victory. In the last four Labour had lost, so while Austin winning in Grimsby had always been a thrill, it had been tempered by sadness and regret at what was happening in the rest of the country. This time Austin's majority was over 16,000. There was no one in the room who had doubted his victory for an instant. Sometimes it seemed such a foregone conclusion, that keeping up the daily grind of canvassing for the six long weeks of the campaign had been hard: walking door-to-door on the council estates; visiting every group dwelling for old people; handing out leaflets in the shopping centre. The little band of supporters had done well to keep it up. Everyone knew a donkey could have won Grimsby this time, provided it wore a Labour rosette.

There was something much more exciting than Labour's victory in Grimsby to celebrate in the Pavilion on the morning of 2 May. The hundreds of young people packing the room let out an enormous cheer as through the door came a tall, slim young woman with a mass of red curls. Several of the men pushed forward and lifted her on to their shoulders. Shona McIsaac, a freelance writer on health and beauty for women's magazines, who had been selected as the Labour candidate for Cleethorpes over two years before, had beaten the Tory MP Michael Brown by more than 9,000 votes.

Shona McIsaac was one of 101 Labour women who became Members of Parliament on 2 May 1997, joining the first Labour government for eighteen years and changing for ever the look and the style of the House of Commons. Suddenly a quarter of Labour Members were women, a fifth of the whole House of Commons.

Shona had been chosen from an all-women shortlist. Cleethorpes was Labour's sixtieth most winnable seat, and the Party had implemented a policy that women must be selected in half the safe and marginal seats. This was the advantage, the kick-start that trade union women, followed by women in the Labour Party, had fought for for over a decade.

The policy had been challenged in the High Court as sexual discrimination by two prospective male candidates before it had been fully implemented. Labour lost the case. After rapid consultation behind the scenes in the Party, Labour decided to keep the advantage it had already won for thirty-eight female candidates and leave the High Court judgement unchallenged.

Angela Eagle, the MP for Wallasey and Environment Minister, a leader in the campaign for all-women shortlists, said she thought the High Court ruling was flawed and could have been overturned, but it was hard work to keep the men at the top of the Party behind the policy, and the women decided to run with the advantage they had already.

For two years Shona McIsaac and other women just like her worked hard in their constituencies, unpaid, unsung heroines of a revolution most voters knew nothing about. Every Friday night, Shona would drive the 200 miles from London

2

to spend the weekend in her chilly Cleethorpes flat. She was always broke. She was often lonely. There was no local Party organisation to speak of. She often spent a whole weekend visiting charity events and chatting about Labour policy to locals without even scoring a mention, let alone a photo in the local paper, the *Grimsby Evening Telegraph*. Meanwhile Austin and the Conservative Michael Brown, the two male MPs for the area, were on front page after front page with the local football team or the diminishing fishing fleet; or sounding off about the Health Service and the local hospital or the area's lack of job prospects.

During the twenty years Austin has been Grimsby's MP, the House of Commons has been very largely male. Women pioneers, often the first in their family to go to university, battled their way through the male bastions to win a tiny proportion of the seats. They were exceptional women and they often shone at Westminster. Barbara Castle, Shirley Williams and Margaret Thatcher herself were the most famous examples. They sat amongst ordinary and extraordinary men, a cross-section of Britain from aristocrats and rich agriculturalists to miners and railway workers. But this was no place for ordinary women – by the very nature of the battle she had fought to get there, any woman who made it to Westminster was a very special person.

The biggest change in 1997 was that the women who were elected, all 120 of them, were a real cross-section of the British public. For the first time there are now nurses and housewives, carers and kindergarten teachers, trade union officials and small businesswomen sitting on the green benches in the House of Commons. Many of them will be stars, some are stars already. Mo Mowlam, Clare Short, Gillian Shephard and Margaret Beckett shine brightly. During this parliament there will doubtless be others. Angela Eagle, Hilary Armstrong and Joan Ruddock are junior Ministers with star quality.

This book is about them. But it is also about Shona McIsaac and all the other ordinary women you have yet to hear about. The women of Westminster, 1997.

I

ORIGIN OF THE SPECIES

IN 1947 SHIRLEY KIRK was the only person in her Sheffield primary school class to pass the eleven plus. Off she went to the grammar school, but not for long. Shirley's parents were poor, they could not afford to buy her a uniform, so they sent her to her new school in her National Health specs and a little pink frock, and hoped for the best. Shirley was the only child in 600 without a uniform. She did her best to ignore the situation and get on with her work, but it was just too much for her. After a couple of weeks she crept away to the secondary modern, where the dress codes were less demanding. She regretted it for the rest of her life.

When Shirley grew up, she married André Eagle, a local lad who had been apprenticed to a printer. They soon moved to Bridlington, where he got his first job. On 17 February 1961 Shirley gave birth to twin daughters, Angela and Maria – destined thirty-six years later to become Britain's first-ever twin Members of Parliament. On 1 May 1997 Maria won Liverpool Garston and joined Angela at Westminster. Angela had prised Wallasey from the Conservatives' grasp in 1992.

The Eagles were remarkable parents, determined to give their children the first-class education which Shirley had been denied. They told them stories about their own tough beginnings, and filled their home with books and newspapers and lively discussions about the world outside. They shared with their children their passion for politics. Maria says that her mother's sad story of her time at the grammar school is one of her earliest memories.

Maria Eagle MP (Labour, Liverpool, Garston): 'This is what politics to me is about, and it affects everyone's lives if politics doesn't work right. My mum was prevented from having a decent education by the accident of birth that her parents didn't have any money.'

Maria Eagle was one of the very few women we spoke to who knew very early in her life that she wanted to be an MP: 'I remember when I was a very young child – I was in an infant school class, so I must have been five or six – and I remember the teacher at the front asking us what we all wanted to be when we grew up. Some little lad said I want to be a fireman and some little girl said I want to be a nurse and I sat in the back thinking I want to be in politics. But I wouldn't have admitted it. I would have been too embarrassed.'

André got a better job and the family moved to Formby in Lancashire when the girls started school, and there they stayed. It was not long before Angela discovered that life was far from plain sailing.

Angela Eagle MP (Labour, Wallasey): 'I discovered when I was eight that it was a problem to be a woman in the world. My dad taught us to play chess and I entered the Formby under-eleven championships. I remember vividly sitting down for my first game, I was drawn against this little boy and he said, "This can't be right, girls don't play chess. I can't be playing you." And it was the first time I had come across this kind of thing. It never occurred to me life might be unfair and I remember saying "But we've been drawn to play against each other," and realising that he was just scared to death I'd beat him and all his friends would laugh at him. I beat him and won the competition. The prize was a Biggles book.'

Already determined to put the world to rights, the Eagles took up professional politics when they were nine.

Maria Eagle: 'It was the 1970 election and we had a mock election at school. We needed a Labour candidate and we tossed up and Angela won. We got battered! We were third, and a poor third as I recall. I helped her write the speech which said that you should vote Labour because of comprehensive education. Given our mother's experience, it seemed obvious . . .'

Angela Eagle: 'We lost because we lived in Formby, which was an incredibly Conservative area and everybody at school just voted the way their parents voted. It was inevitable.'

Only a few other female Members of Parliament saw themselves as potential politicians when they were children. Clare Curtis-Thomas had the clearest vision.

Claire Curtis-Thomas MP (Labour, Crosby): 'I remember the funeral of Winston Churchill in 1963. It was in black and white on the TV and it was incredibly sombre. I can remember seeing the Houses of Parliament for the first time. I knew from a very young age that was what I wanted to do. My mother tells me I was always objecting to wrongs on other people's behalf. I was always interested in other people's welfare and social conditions. Mum used to say I'd have to talk for a living.

'I saw being an MP as a platform to articulate other issues – not just for the sake of it. I've never been anything for a title. I have always enjoyed positions because of what they can achieve.'

Oona King also knew she wanted to be a politician, but she wasn't planning to stay on the backbenches.

Oona King MP (Labour, Bethnal Green and Bow): 'I decided I wanted to be Prime Minister at about the age of four and I outgrew that ambition by the age of twelve. I always wanted to be a politician. There are some people who always know they want to be a dancer, or a writer or a fireman. I just knew what I wanted.'

Diane Abbott found herself sorting out the world's problems before she went to school in the morning.

Diane Abbott MP (Labour, Hackney North and Stoke Newington): 'My mother would plait my hair while she listened to the Home Service news on the radio. Hearing about political events, strikes and so on I was thinking to myself "Well, if I was Prime Minister I would do this, if I was Prime Minister I would do that." I must have been about eight or nine.'

If you have a daughter and you would like her to grow up to be an MP, your chances will be greatly improved if you are in politics yourself. <u>Over half the present female Members of Parliament come from families with strong political connections.</u> The strongest connection of all is the father. If he was an MP or a councillor or active in his Party locally and his daughter spent precious hours of her childhood helping him deliver leaflets or canvassing, talking politics with him, and preferably arguing vociferously within the family, then a lifelong interest in politics would often result.

An outstanding example of this singular passion for politics is the Leader of the House, Ann Taylor. Aged twenty-seven when she became an MP, she'd already been a Labour Party member for thirteen years. When we talked together about her life in youth politics, she mentioned getting married ('We ran the Young Socialists between us and it seemed the sensible thing to do') as if it had been just another step on a lifelong political journey which began when she was a little girl in Bolton, accompanying her father as he toured the town.

Rt Hon. Ann Taylor MP (Labour, Dewsbury): 'My father had been interested in politics all his life. He used to go round knocking on doors at local elections as well as general elections, collecting subs, delivering news letters or notices for meetings. I used to go with him when I was eight or nine and I can remember listening to him having arguments and not being quite sure whether this was right, and then getting interested in what he was talking about.

'When I went to secondary school, I went to a girl's direct grant school on a scholarship from a council estate, so I was in a very small minority. Probably a minority of one, in terms of being politically active or interested from a Labour point of view. And then we had a very important election in Bolton when I was thirteen, when the old Liberal-Conservative pact broke down in the town. My father was helping quite a bit and I was old enough to know about what was going on. And at school it was considered proper that "good gals" should have some civic awareness. You were supposed to know what was going on. I either had to keep my head down and keep quiet, or know more about politics than anyone else.

'I had my first Party card when I was fourteen. You were supposed to be fifteen. I always looked older than I was. We had an active Young Socialists. It was a good atmosphere. Positive and exciting and camaraderie and everyone working together. It was my social life as well as my political life.'

The Speaker, Betty Boothroyd, like Ann Taylor put her love of politics above everything else.

'I'm an only child, and my parents were involved in the Labour Party in the West Riding in Yorkshire but not very high-profile people. I joined the Labour Party at the age of sixteen in what was then the Labour League of Youth.

'Until I became Speaker I had been in the Labour Party all my life. It was great fun actually, I thoroughly enjoyed it – we were very active. We visited other people's constituencies. We went to political rallies. We went to all the by-elections.We went on hikes on the moors. We had a lot of fun hiking and debating and meeting in each others' houses and moving around with cheap coach fares to the countryside and to the seaside.'

Five members had fathers who were MPs when they were growing up.

Hilary Armstrong (Labour, North West Durham): 'My father stood for parliament when I was about eight or nine the first time and was unsuccessful. So I remember that. I remember the first election address – the only address the family was ever on. We took a collective decision that we didn't want to do that. My mum was very clear about it. She would support him, but we were not standing for election.'

Hilary Armstrong's father became the Labour MP for North West Durham in 1963. He stayed until 1987, when Hilary became the first-ever woman member to replace her father. Like Maria Eagle, she was affected by education policies.

'The event that probably had the most influence on me was the move to comprehensive education. When I was in secondary school, my father won the chairmanship of the Education Committee in Sunderland, on the basis that he would take the town comprehensive, and I was at the grammar school. I remember all the debates and arguments. We would have them at home and I would go and listen to them in the council chamber, and I used to get the backlash at school. The English teacher was so angry about it – he used to lecture the class that my father wanted to "let the clots into the cream". I was once made to kneel on a coconut mat while he expounded the evils of comprehensive education to the class.'

Llin Golding replaced her husband as the MP for Newcastle-under-Lyme, but her dad had been a Member too.

Llin Golding MP (Labour, Newcastle-under-Lyme): 'The fact that my father was an MP had a large influence on me because politics were always talked about in our house. He was here at Westminster all during the last war, so it was a very interesting time and certainly got me interested in politics.

'All the family have been involved at some point in time. My brothers are in the local Party. My twin sister stood for parliament herself, but didn't get in. Many of the family have been involved in parish councils, district councils and county councils. I've got distant relatives who have been MPs, and my husband was an MP.'

Charlotte Atkins MP (Labour, Staffordshire Moorlands): 'I worked in the 1959 election, when I was nine, collecting numbers; I come from a very political background. Born into politics actually. My father stood for Lowestoft in 1964, and Maldon, his local seat, in 1966. He lost it by about three votes and got selected for Preston North in a very odd selection: he was the only person on the shortlist who wasn't sponsored, and he only had one nomination – from the Young Socialists, which is normally the kiss of death. He was asked a very racist question "What would you do if your daughter was going out with a black man?" and I think in fact I was at the time and he blew his top, got the selection and became an MP when I was sixteen. Although he's now in his eighties, he is still a councillor in Preston.'

Dari Taylor MP (Labour, Stockton South): 'In the 1959

election, my father was fighting a safe seat in Burnley, Lancashire. I have a lasting memory of some of the most astounding characters in politics. Macmillan saying, "You've never had it so good", and six hundred thousand out of work. And the excitement of my father winning. The count. Waiting. That sense of anticipation. Not believing that he'd won until they announced the figures. I think that probably, all put together, it had a profound effect on me.'

Dari Taylor was one of many women who mentioned the excitement and pleasure the family took in political arguments. She could hardly wait for her dad to get back from Westminster at the end of each week.

'We missed him tremendously. He added colour. We all used to wait for Friday when he came home and each of us had our different versions of what he should have done during the week over various policies.

'My mother, seeing how exhausted he used to become, would say, "When he comes home today you don't mention politics, not one word!" But he hadn't been home half an hour and we were into it. And it wasn't a bit of a surprise to any of them when I went to university to read politics.'

Ray Michie MP (Liberal Democrat, Argyll and Bute): 'I come from a political family. My father was a Liberal peer. I grew up with Liberalism. One of my first memories is campaigning with him, going around knocking on doors, being with him at public meetings, which were always enormous in those days. He took me around a lot on his campaigns. I was also able to take my mother's place at various things, if she wasn't able to go. When I was seventeen or eighteen, I remember going to Dublin to meet the President of Ireland.'

Janet Anderson's dad wasn't quite so grand. He was a Labour Party agent in Jarrow.

Janet Anderson MP (Labour, Rossendale and Darwen): 'He was Hugh Dalton's agent for many years. I remember Barbara Castle coming to our front door when she came to speak at a meeting there. I'd have been about seven I suppose. They had a very big Labour club there. You still had quite large meetings and I remember helping my dad set out chairs for public meetings, and then we used to fold them up afterwards. I have this memory of them all having chewing gum stuck to the bottom.

'I remember the 1964 election. We'd moved to Bristol, my father was an agent in Bristol then, going to hear Harold Wilson speak and coming away so enthusiastic. Asking my head teacher whether I could have the day off to help with the election and she said no, but a group of us took it anyway, and we all got detention when we got back.'

Several other women had fathers and sometimes mothers who were political enthusiasts and passed on their passion to their daughters. Cheryl Gillan (Conservative, Chesham and Amersham) remembers selling raffle tickets at Party events attended by her parents, and sometimes even making the draw. Eleanor Laing (Conservative, Epping Forest) has memories of helping her father in his campaign to be elected as a local councillor in 1966. She was only six or seven, but she helped out nevertheless. Jean Corston (Labour, Bristol East), Anne McGuire (Labour, Stirling), Helen Brinton (Labour, Peterborough), and Anne Begg (Labour, Aberdeen South) all tell similar stories of helping activist parents to stuff envelopes and deliver them.

Ann Keen is another new member with strong political connections. Her husband, Alan Keen MP represents the seat next door to hers. Her sister, Sylvia Heal, is the member for Halesowen and Rowley Regis.

Ann Keen MP (Labour, Brentford and Isleworth): 'My father was a councillor and a trade union steward in the steel works, and always had the local MP round the house helping with surgeries, and the MP was a woman – Eirene White, now Baroness White. So of course for me to see a woman as a Member of Parliament wasn't strange. At election time the house was a committee room and I'd run with the members in the polling stations, giving out leaflets. My three-wheeler bike, the boot stuffed with leaflets. So for Sylvia and I, it's in our dreams. Our two brothers, who were younger than us, could not be less interested if they tried.'

Women who came from strongly political families often

mentioned with pleasure that arguing politics had been an important childhood experience. Judy Mallaber (Labour, Amber Valley) remembers there being a great deal of political argument because her parents supported different parties. Her father was a Labour agent in 1945; her mother, who was a solid traditional Liberal, came from the Welsh borders in Shropshire, pure Liberal territory. 'I was brought up with lots of political arguments in the household. I grew up with that going on. My sister is quite argumentative too.'

Anne Campbell (Labour, Cambridge) had similar experiences, with an 'old fashioned liberal . . . right wing' father and a mother who was a member of the Conservative Party. 'Fierce arguments all the time. That's the sort of background I was brought up in.' Judith Church (Labour, Dagenham) remembers 1966 (she thinks) when her mother voted Labour, and there was a huge uproar in the house about it when she eventually confessed her electoral crime to Judith's father. 'My father was proved right and my mother was proved wrong,' she maintains. 'It was a mistake to have voted for a Labour government. I grew up in a very Tory household.' The political split proved to be a sign of something deeper, and her parents were eventually divorced. Judith stayed with her mother.

Joan Ruddock's (Labour, Lewisham, Deptford) father was a supervisor in a factory. She recalls that, when there was a strike, she 'went off and tried to talk to the shop stewards' – not to help her father, but 'because I wondered why they were doing it'.

If there is a Labour Party aristocracy, then Gwyneth Dunwoody is part of it. Her father, Morgan Phillips, was made General Secretary of the Labour Party in 1960. Her mother was a life peer and her grandmother was a famous suffragette.

Hon. Gwyneth Dunwoody MP (Labour, Crewe and Nantwich): 'I went everywhere with my parents because there's nine years between myself and my brother, so I was like an only child, and everything they did, I did. The first Labour Party conference I went to, I must have been about three . . . it makes me smile now when they talk about a crêche because I was always entertained, there were always large numbers of Labour ladies sitting around who were delighted to entertain you.'

Gwyneth grew up and married Dr John Dunwoody, who was just as keen on politics as she was. They became Members of Parliament at the same election. 'If everybody in the family is in politics, one grows used to the idea that during an election, it is your duty to stick leaflets through doors and knock on doors. It seems to be a kind of gentle progression from this stage towards full-blown political involvement.'

In a very few families, women seemed to be the dominant force, and in one, Virginia Bottomley's, women have been involved in public life and politics across the spectrum. Her cousin, Baroness Jay, is a Labour Minister.

Rt Hon. Virginia Bottomley MP (Conservative, South West Surrey): 'I come from a political family which consists of many forceful women both on my side and on Peter's,' (her husband, Peter Bottomley MP). 'My aunt, Peggy Jay, was a tremendous champion of the old LCC, she was a magistrate, she gave me great encouragement, and I think she was what we now call a role model. My great-aunt founded Northern Ladies' College.

'My mother-in-law wasn't able to continue her career in the way she would have liked, but I have no doubt that was one of the reasons she gave me unequivocal support.'

Jenny Jones (Labour, Wolverhampton South West) recalls a working-class Tory household where women were the powerful figures. They were the people who discussed the affairs of the day and gave out the opinions. The men, on the other hand, she remembers, used to sidle off to the allotment sheds or in her dad's case, go fishing. A vivid early memory for Jenny is the 1951 general election, when her father was very upset at the result, which swung from Labour back to Tory.

When her parents' marriage broke up, and Jenny endured the privations and the stigma attached to one-parent families in the 1950s (her mother pretended she was a widow), she began to develop opinions of her own: 'I began to think – hang on a minute – she worked hard, we were on low incomes and this ethos, this system which her and my grandmother were banging on about, simply didn't work. I benefited from the education system of the Labour government . . . eventually I began to think there was a much better way of doing things.'

Tessa Jowell (Labour, Dulwich and West Norwood) was also influenced by her mother, a Quaker, 'She believed that all people have an intrinsic worth.' Jowell believes she has inherited this: 'That's why I feel so passionate about what exclusion does.'

Jacqui Smith (Labour, Redditch), the daughter of two local councillors, remembers going to 10 Downing Street with her mother, and being deeply impressed. Her mother, especially, acted as a role model. 'She did stand for selection for parliamentary seats and I think she would have done a very good job . . . it was partly symptomatic of the changes in the Labour Party that she was unsuccessful and I was successful.'

The 1945 election, which Labour won with a landslide, obviously made the nation very interested and excited. For several of the older women members who were tiny children at the time, it was an important early memory. Alice Mahon (Labour, Halifax) remembers the ecstasy and the expectation of the Labour victory: 'I can remember the men who had come home from the war and the expectation was that when the Health Service came in, everything would change for ever.' Her experiences of the pre-Welfare State, she told me, were formative. 'When the men were away, my older sister had been ill with scarlet fever and the women had had to have a whip-round to get the doctor to come out, and I remember her being taken away, wrapped in a red blanket.'

Rt Hon. Gillian Shephard MP (Conservative, South West Norfolk): 'I remember the Labour Party winning in 1945 and people running up and down the street in our village shouting "They're in! They're in!" and I remember a great pall of despair settling on our household. I was five, I couldn't think why this might be. I said, "What is it?", and they said,

"They've got rid of Mr Churchill", which made me think, "Have they drowned him? Have they shot him?" and sensing an enormous feeling of injustice in our household over what they'd done to Mr Churchill.'

Many of the younger women said it was a sense of injustice, an awareness of unfairness in their daily lives that started their interest in politics. Gillian Merron (Labour, Lincoln) attended schools where there were sharp differences between the haves and the have-nots. 'If I saw injustice to other children I would say something. I felt conscious of the fact that I was going to a school where lots of the children were better off than us. I was aware of the differences. Aware that it would be harder for me.' Rosie Winterton (Labour, Doncaster Central) also established a reputation for standing up to prejudice. 'You would see people being bullied because they were poor or their fathers were out of work and they just had that generally underprivileged look about them. I used to stand up to the bullies.'

Dr Lynne Jones MP (Labour, Birmingham, Selly Oak): 'I remember from quite an early age feeling there was a lot of unfairness. I was brought up on a council estate, my father suffered from mental illness, my mother was the breadwinner. I could see my mother working really hard and the standard of living we had was really poor. I just thought things were unfair. That's what got me interested in politics.'

Hazel Blears MP (Labour, Salford): 'I have a clear memory of being out with my mother, aged ten or eleven, shopping in Manchester and seeing a tramp literally delving in baskets looking for something to eat. It was really quite a shock – the first time I had come up against that situation and realised that some people didn't have enough to eat. I was very upset about it. From that time I became quite concerned that something had to be done so that people didn't live like that.'

Beverley Hughes MP (Labour, Stretford and Urmston): 'The kind of values I learned from my family were about justice and injustice. At grammar school in my first year, it was co-educational, dinner times were horrendous because every table had these monitors who shared out the food; and

15

I remember those boys at the head of the table who used to take half a tin of whatever it was for themselves and share the other half of the tin amongst the other six people at the table and I can remember being absolutely incensed by this. I didn't think twice about it, I stood up and took the tin and was going to take it to the teacher and these boys took it back and shared it out.'

In a way, this was a kind of self-discovery, an individualised version of the old-style socialist ideals Audrey Wise (Labour, Preston) grew up with: 'I was born into a family in which it was taken for granted that everyone took an interest in the community. I was brought up to think society was vital and that you couldn't have a satisfactory life yourself unless you were contributing to that for everybody.'

Some women who came from non-political backgrounds were awakened to the possibility of a political career by schoolteachers who opened new doors on the world. The Northern Ireland Secretary, Mo Mowlam, is the daughter of a postman father and a telephonist mother. She went to school in Coventry.

Rt Hon. Mo Mowlam MP (Labour, Redcar): 'The first political influences were teachers at school who made me think about issues. I liked school, did well at the local comprehensive – I was head girl. Miss Morley was the teacher who was important. She inspired me. She said, "You can do what you want. Go for it. If you work hard, you can get there."

'We still talk about her. There are girls I keep up with from school, and we all did vaguely different things but we all stood up for what we wanted. There's a lovely story of Miss Morley. I went to do a public meeting in Bournemouth where she's retired and Miss Morley was sitting there in the front row in her pill-box hat and suit in turquoise. She stood out sitting there, but she'd come to see me because I was hers. Now I may not have been of her politics, but she was the first one that made me think. Made me actually analyse and discuss and debate.'

Christine Russell MP (Labour, City of Chester): 'I'm a

farmer's daughter from rural Lincolnshire. My village school-teacher was the wife of the leader of the Farmworkers' Union. There was always a very strong social dimension. It wasn't just about battles in history lessons. I remember her taking us on a school outing to a village school in Norfolk where there was actually a schools' strike in 1906. At the time it didn't register, but I think that's where I got this sense of injustice. That was the one thing I had to do . . . to fight the injustice of it all.'

Karen Buck (Labour, Regent's Park and Kensington North) is a self-confessed Essex girl and the only child of a single-parent family. She recalls being struck by the three-day week and the miners' strike of 1973–4. 'It just opened my eyes to a fascinating world and I was completely riveted by it. I remember thinking, "This is what I want to study. This is what I want to know about."' An economics teacher provided her with encouragement. 'I remember her saying to me, when I was about fifteen, "You're interested in politics. You should be an MP," and thinking, "Don't be so stupid."'

For three people, the eleven-plus shaped the rest of their lives and gave them a political start.

Joan Walley MP (Labour, Stoke-on-Trent North): 'I sat my eleven-plus in the year the new grammar school was opened. It offered a whole range of extra-curricular activities, there was suddenly a whole new horizon. In the second year, I set up a social services committee which got wallpapering done for old people and gardening and a whole load of different things. The headmaster asked me if I would like to make a speech at the Christmas carol service to raise money for the social services society and I refused and said I couldn't possibly because I was too nervous and shy. He talked me into it. I felt ill for a week before but I actually did it.'

Shona McIsaac MP (Labour, Cleethorpes): 'My dad was stationed in NATO HQ in Belgium and when we got back to Britain I was thirteen. Because I'd missed the eleven-plus, the Education Authority just said she goes to the local secondary modern. It was such a shock. There was such a culture of "them and us" between the people at the secondary modern school and the people at the grammar school and that made me feel there was a lot of unfairness around. In the end I did get transferred to the high school, it had an arson attack, and then I saw it from the other side. That was a very strange experience, having gone to both and seen the divisions it created.'

Ann Cryer MP (Labour, Keighley): 'I was told I'd failed my eleven-plus and all my friends had passed. I never really got over it, because all my friends went to the grammar school. I knew that I was cleverer than some of them, I felt as if I had been cheated.'

Two of the new women Members, who are in their fifties, were proud of the influence of the New Towns on their politics:

Eileen Gordon MP (Labour, Romford): 'My parents moved out of the East End of London after the war to Howard's Hill, which was a London County Council estate in Essex. We came from a tenement block and we were given a three-bedroom house with two loos. It was like the countryside. It was a new estate and I went to a new school. My deep commitment to the Welfare State and the NHS comes because I benefited from it.'

Laura Moffatt (Labour, Crawley) was similarly influenced by her parents' move from south London to Crawley. The New Towns, she declares with conviction, 'produced people like me'.

Not surprisingly, the new Members in their twenties and thirties were all in one way or another influenced by Margaret Thatcher.

Lorna Fitzsimons MP (Labour, Rochdale) has an early memory of Mrs Thatcher: 'When Margaret Thatcher got elected, I've got an image of her standing on the stairway of Central Office waving to the world in a flowery dress. My mum and dad were thinking doom and gloom, a bad day for British politics.

'I joined the Labour Party when I moved away from Rochdale and went to a small art college at Loughborough, and the first wave of cuts in higher education meant that they tried to shut my college down and I became aware of national government policy and how it impinged on my life, so I started to get involved.'

Ruth Kelly's (Labour, Bolton West) first political memory is of Margaret Thatcher being elected Prime Minister in 1979. At that point in her life – she was eleven years old – she was very pleased to see a woman getting that far in politics. Thatcher's election convinced the young Ruth Kelly that it was important for her to make it as a woman, as well as an individual. 'I could see from my mother's generation the obstacles they faced, so I was very aware of the different routes that were presented to boys and girls from the earliest moments of their lives.'

In the 1950s, televisions were turned on in living-rooms across the land, and this opened up the world to some idealistic young British women who found their political inspiration in other countries.

Joan Humble MP (Labour, Blackpool North and Fleetwood): 'For me it was John Kennedy, President of America, saying to people, "Ask not what your country can do for you, but rather what you can do for your country." There was a lot of hope then, people really thinking they could change the world for the better. I was the first member of my family to go to university and I saw improvements in my parents' lifestyle, in my opportunities, so my politics are based on hope for the future.'

Gisela Stuart MP (Labour, Birmingham Edgbaston) was born and brought up in Germany and recalls the Prague Spring of 1968: 'I was in Bavaria – it was the August school holidays and we were sitting glued to the radio. We had family over in Czechoslovakia and we knew some refugee friends who were coming up via Austria, and that was probably the most politicising event. My mother was a refugee from Eastern Europe: you have an awareness of political events if they affect your life so directly.'

Margaret Ewing MP (Scottish Nationalist, Moray): 'My first-ever political action was writing to the *Daily Record* when I was maybe about twelve. It was about apartheid in

South Africa and I think I actually got a five shilling postal order, because those were the days when people paid you to write letters.'

Kali Mountford MP (Labour, Colne Valley): 'I remember being very upset about the famine in Biafra. I was very conscious of famines all over the place. Dreadful things happening to people and I thought it wasn't right. I also have strong memories of Mandela being arrested and going to prison. I did a course at school called Government and Citizenship and I just thought it was inspirational: the realisation that this was how you changed things, and no amount of moaning would work, that you had to do it yourself.'

Melanie Johnson MP (Labour, Welwyn Hatfield) was struck by the assassination of Martin Luther King, but also moved by events closer to home. 'We had an inside toilet, but quite a lot of the other children didn't. They had toilets down the end of gardens and I remember being struck by the difference in their lives and my life.'

Linda Gilroy MP (Labour Co-operative, Plymouth Sutton): 'The Hungarian uprising, which was 1956. I was about seven. I remember getting very upset and writing a letter and posting it in a postbox. I forget who the letter was to, but somebody. I thought somebody would do something about it.'

Diana Organ (Labour, Forest of Dean) also recalls being moved by the famine in Biafra, while Valerie Davey's (Labour, Bristol West) political watershed was teaching in Tanzania in the 1960s. 'I saw for the first time a very poor country exploited by wealthy countries.' Bridget Prentice (Labour, Lewisham East) was similarly affected by Third World events. Her first political action was to write a letter to Nelson Mandela when she was about ten. 'I didn't think I was being political. I just thought it was terrible that he was being imprisoned.'

Rt Hon. Clare Short MP (Labour, Birmingham, Ladywood) was showing future promise for her role as International Development Secretary when she was at primary school: 'During the Suez crisis, I was ten, and in the playground all the children were singing "We'll throw Nasser in the Suez Canal", and I got the whole class to stop and come round and explained to them it was wrong and this canal was in Egypt and people were allowed to have their own canal.

'That was the same year as the Russian invasion of Hungary and my father used to stick things on the wall. He was that kind of person. We were a left-wing family but we all knew what the Russians did was completely wrong. On the other hand, we didn't think that Britain was right in Suez. We just grew up with values like that.'

At least five women grew up abroad. Gisela Stuart is German and came to Britain to work in a bookshop when she was a teenager. Margaret Hodge was born in Egypt, the child of German-Austrian refugees. She came to England when she was five, her family were stateless and could not obtain a visa to go anywhere else. The family was Jewish, and Margaret's father had the children christened in the hope that it would help them gain British citizenship.

Margaret Hodge MP (Labour, Barking): 'My mother died when I was ten and I became an impossible teenager. I was the middle one of five and my father couldn't cope with me, so he sent me off to Oxford High School. My sister was at university there at the time and that's when class, the British class system, hit me, because I was sent to this school where half the kids there had passed the eleven-plus, and their parents worked at the Morris car factory, and the other half were upper-class people who got there because they paid, and never the twain shall mix. I felt an uncomfortable misfit and very angry with the class system.'

Three other Members were educated on the other side of the world. Patricia Hewitt is Australian, and Chris McCafferty and Roseanna Cunningham's parents emigrated there to give their families a better chance.

Patricia Hewitt MP (Labour, Leicester West): 'My father was a very senior public servant in Australia. I remember him refusing to tell me how he voted, and he never has to this day. He was ultra-secretive on anything official. My mum was in various forms of voluntary work and my grandmother had been quite an active suffragette, and then she'd gone out to Australia and discovered, in a sense to her disappointment, that women already had the vote in Australia. She was the first woman elected to the Hospital Board, and she served on a whole array of public and voluntary organisations. I got active in campaigning as a schoolgirl.'

Chris McCafferty MP (Labour, Calder Valley) was back in Britain by her late teens. Her parents hadn't been able to settle: 'When we returned, getting off the ship at Tilbury, it was a very bad winter. Everything seemed dirty, shabby, very cold. I remember being on the boat train from Tilbury to London looking out the windows, halfway back to Manchester, and I was just appalled at the housing most of the people were living in. Over in Australia, even in the Fifties, most people lived in bungalows, with a good half acre of land. They all had fitted cupboards in the bedrooms, fitted wardrobes, fitted kitchens. Coming back here was a huge shock.

'I went back briefly to Whalley Range Girls' High, but I didn't fit in any more. The head was very scathing about Australian academic qualifications – the reckoning was that while it was a very strict girls' grammar school, I was naïve by comparison to all those girls I'd left so many years before.'

For Roseanna Cunningham, the situation was almost the opposite. From the minute she arrived in Australia she dreamed about Scotland, her country.

Roseanna Cunningham MP (Scottish Nationalist, Perth): 'I decided when I went out there that I was coming back. I was eight and I made up my mind I was coming back to Scotland, standing on the ship as it left Southampton. I hung on to that very hard and worked very hard at learning about Scotland.

'When I was sixteen I wrote to the SNP for the first time and asked if they would send stuff.'

Roseanna Cunningham stayed in Australia for seventeen years. She was twenty-five when she completed her politics honours degree at the University of Western Australia. Then she went home to Scotland.

The background and the political beginnings of the 120 female Members of Parliament elected on 1 May is broad.

There are women from every corner of Britain ranging in age from twenty-four to sixty-six. There are doctors, nurses, lawyers, trade union officers, councillors, teachers, lecturers, journalists, carers and an engineer. Over half of them come from families that are strongly political and one in eight have relatives who are, or have been Members.

Fathers, particularly, have been strong role models, but this is hardly surprising. These women were born at a time when MPs, except for a tiny few, were men. All professional jobs were dominated by men; only now are things beginning to change. It is the children of these women members who will be worth watching. Can MP mothers make it as role models for their daughters like MP fathers did? Twenty years from now will Hannah, daughter of Caroline Flint MP, be following in Mummy's footsteps, or taking a secretarial job and bringing up a family, just like her dad?

2

INTO PARLIAMENT SHE MUST GO

AND SO THEY ARRIVED at Westminster in the first week of May 1997, 120 bright-eyed British daughters. Smart, well educated, experienced in the ways of the world. Many of them came from political families, so they had been dealing with politics and politicians all their lives. Many had been councillors, council leaders, teachers, heads, senior doctors, lawyers, barristers, journalists, consultants, carers and mothers. Had they planned then to be Members of Parliament as the next step on a well-constructed career ladder? Turned childhood dreams into reality? Good heavens no, the thought had never occurred to them. Nearly all the women protested modestly that the idea of being an MP had never entered their heads.

'It was people in Blackburn who made me do it,' Janet Anderson, Vice-Chamberlain in Her Majesty's Household, said hastily. Her colleague, Assistant Whip Bridget Prentice, went further, denying she had so much as even thought about being an MP until one or two of her women friends had suggested it. Her immediate reaction was, 'What would I want to do that for?' Anne Begg had similar doubts. 'Various people had said, "Why not stand for Westminster?", and I said, "No, the last thing I want to do is go down to this old boys' club."' According to Anne Campbell, 'Somebody put my name on the list for MP selection and I almost took it off again.'

Betty Boothroyd, the Speaker, was one of the only women who admitted that, as a bright young spark, she wanted to push herself forward. She was working as a secretary at the

House of Commons first to Sir Geoffrey de Freitas and then to Barbara Castle.

'Well, I love politics, I enjoy my politics and of course I fell in love with not just the House but what is done here. I take great pride in the way democracy functions and I thought well here I am working here behind the throne for a couple of Members and I thought, I can do as well as they can! I thought, I can do that! I wasn't looking for a safe seat or anything – you've got to cut your teeth in this life. I said to the Labour Party that I wanted to be on one of their candidate lists. They said "Oh you're too young you want to get a bit of age on your shoulders first." It was a man called Williams – Len Williams, Secretary General of the Labour Party – who said put some age on your shoulders first, but I didn't get age on my shoulders I got a bit of experience and I took on a seat, South East Leicester, which had a twenty thousand majority and that was my first attempt.'

One in five of the 120 women MPs explained how she would never have stood had it not been for somebody else's intervention. Of the 76 Labour women I spoke to, only 27 admitted they had put their own names forward. And a significant number of those still seemed uncomfortable that they had done so. Clare Short described putting her name forward for the list in her local constituency, Battersea, as 'purely excruciating'. 'The hardest thing I ever did in the whole of my political career was to say I'd like to be one,' she told me. 'I was so ashamed of promoting myself in this way.' After trying a number of nominations and selections, she was finally elected by the voters of Birmingham Ladywood in 1983.

Compared with this, Candy Atherton (Labour, Falmouth and Camborne) seems almost shockingly ambitious. Over coffee in the Pugin Room, she told me how, without really thinking it through, she put her name forward towards the end of the selection processes for the 1992 election and found her phone ringing full-time as constituencies invited her for interview. In 1997 she took it all more seriously and was networking to be selected in one of the Swindon seats when Falmouth and Camborne came up. Her selection there was controversial: a local Party member believed the seat was his, but the Party had voted for an all-women shortlist.

Describing the acrimonious battle this man and a few of his friends in the Labour Party stirred up, she suddenly interrupted herself and asked, 'Can I go back a bit? I mean it implies that I sort of fell into being a parliamentary candidate.' She wanted to set the record straight. She told me being an MP was something she would have always wanted to do. 'I'm a great believer in – if you want to do something, do it yourself.'

Short and Atherton are from different generations, of course. The political culture of the Labour Party had changed in the decade and a half between their stories, and so had women, however slow the progress through the glass ceiling. Party research in 1992 found that approximately 20 per cent of local Labour councillors were women, a significant and growing number. Including the former Mayor of Islington, Atherton herself, almost half of Labour's sixty-four new women MPs gained political experience through their involvement in local politics. And half of these admitted to having actively looked for a parliamentary seat.

Jane Griffiths remembers selection time in Reading East in 1995, trying to think about what the right candidate for the constituency would be like. 'As I narrowed it down, I seemed to narrow it down to myself, really.' According to Melanie Johnson (Labour, Welwyn Hatfield), 'It was obviously the next step.' For Phyllis Starkey (Labour, Milton Keynes South West) there was nothing else to do in local government, so she tried for selection in her home constituency. It was an unwinnable seat for Labour. Even so, things did not go according to plan. 'I wasn't selected and I was so annoyed that I thought I'm going to get selected for a seat I'm going to win. I'm going to show people that I can be an MP.'

But women like Atherton, Griffiths, Johnson, and Starkey are the exceptions. Most of the 1997 intake still describe their journey to Westminster with profound ambivalence. There seem to be three main reasons why. First, there is the old problem of not wanting to be accused of looking after number one. Geraldine Smith found the transition from local government to prospective parliamentary candidate very hard.

Geraldine Smith (Labour, Morecambe and Lunesdale): 'I'd been a councillor and everything but I didn't want to appear a careerist. It seems daft, after being in the Labour Party seventeen years – if I'd been a careerist, I'd have come straight in and looked around for seats. It was just telling people that you wanted to go for it and telling all your friends within the Party.'

Even those women who had put themselves forward seemed to feel the need to justify such an unseemly act of self-advancement. 1997 was the third time Hazel Blears stood as a parliamentary candidate and if anyone should know why they want to be an MP, it is her: 'In a way the Labour Party that I know, although it is changing to some extent, is a party where you gradually take steps, and you become more skilled and more able and more proficient at representing people. And I suppose the heart of being able to represent people is in parliament. But it's all the same motivation, it's the same driving force.'

Lorna Fitzsimons told me she had never wanted to be an MP. 'I still don't want to be an MP, an MP is a means to an end. I really disagree with people who want to be MPs.' So does Geraldine Smith. 'I didn't join the Labour Party and think, I want to be an MP. I joined the Labour Party and thought, I want to change things, I want to change the world.' Self-promotion doesn't mix easily with socialism, not even the watered-down socialism of Blair's New Labour.

Then there is the problem of poor public image. According to a pre-election survey, politicians are now even less popular than journalists. Of course, you should not believe what you read in the newspapers, and anyone on the inside of national politics will tell you that they know plenty of decent, intelligent, hard-working MPs, but that is not the point. Jacqui Smith told me she had always quite fancied the idea of being an MP, but never said as much out loud. 'I think if you're eighteen and you've just started at university and you tell everybody you want to be an MP . . . you're going to lose all your friends, aren't you?'

Judy Mallaber and Karen Buck both swore they would never be MPs. Judy Mallaber: 'I'm not one of those people who had an ambition. One of my competitors in my selection said she had always wanted to be an MP. But it had never occurred to me that that was a great ambition.' Karen Buck decided to stand for selection incredibly late: 'That's why I'd never trust a politician really, because I'd always said you wouldn't catch me doing that with a barge pole. Anybody who wants to do it should be disbarred.'

Hardened politicians might argue that if you cannot stand up to the cynicism and prejudice of your contemporaries you should not be in politics at all. But, as the Conservative Party discovered to their detriment on 2 May, the line between having a healthy disregard for opinion polls and completely losing touch with the electorate is very thin. MPs, Labour MPs especially, are supposed to listen to people: they are, after all, our representatives. Unfortunately the best listeners tend by definition to be more sensitive to criticism and no one likes to be unpopular. This ties in with the final, principal, reason for women MPs' political ambivalence: confidence, something women from all the parties own up to suffering a lack of now and then.

Eleanor Laing remembers telling her teacher what she wanted to be when she grew up. 'I might have been thirteen, but anyhow I was very young. I said, "A politician," and he laughed. And over the following week in lots of classes that I went to, teachers made remarks about me wanting to be a politician and they were all laughing at me. I've never forgotten it.'

According to Julie Kirkbride (Conservative, Bromsgrove), 'It does take a lot of confidence to stand, because there are a lot of brickbats around. So you've got to feel pretty robust about yourself and about the people who would be hurt by the criticism of you.'

Little did Jackie Ballard know, when she first wrote to Paddy Ashdown back in 1983 discussing 'various different things that were bothering me locally', that she would end up

Member of Parliament for Taunton and Liberal Democrat spokesperson for women: 'After a fairly long series of letters back and forward and phone calls and things, he turned up on my doorstep and said, "Look, you're obviously a Liberal, why don't you join the party and get involved?" Without being sycophantic, if it wasn't for Paddy Ashdown encouraging me to go on that track I would never have got here. Women do need to be encouraged, I think. It's a truism.'

Clare Short told me she 'would never have dreamed in a thousand million years of someone like me being an MP'. Thirteen years her junior, Angela Smith (Labour Co-operative, Basildon) agreed. 'If you said to me when I was seventeen that I'd be doing this now, I would have hid under the bedcovers and never got out again. People like me don't become MPs.'

Janet Anderson said, 'I used to sit in political meetings, thinking, "I'd really like to make this point, but I'm not sure, it might sound silly, and I know someone's probably said it before." And I used to develop a nervous twitch at the back of my neck. But gradually I realised it's never stopped men. They are determined to say their bit, regardless of whether it's relevant or whether it's been said before. And I say to women all the time, and I say to my daughter, it is all about confidence. There is no reason in the world why you can't do it.'

The best defence both against insecurity and the accusation of 'careerism' is to pick a constituency and stick to it. The closer to home the better. Hilary Armstrong was the natural candidate for North West Durham, her father's old seat. Llin Golding and Ann Cryer replaced their husbands. And both Laura Moffatt and Linda Perham were councillors, then Mayors, of their respective constituencies, Crawley and Ilford North. Like Anderson, and Conservative Member for Congleton, Ann Winterton, they were not about to go touting themselves around the country looking for alternatives. 'I wasn't interested in any other seat,' said Perham. Moffatt agreed. 'I wasn't going anywhere else.' Moffatt and Anderson nursed their seats through more than one election, as did all three Liberal Democrats. Ray Michie's seat had been a Tory stronghold since the 1920s, and when she first arrived, the Liberal association was in a state of collapse. In 1979 she stood against John Mackay (now Lord Mackay of Ardbrecknish) a former Liberal candidate who switched to the Conservatives.

Ray Michie: 'I was fourth but I held my deposit. I came second at the next election, then I won the third time. It took a lot of nursing and, because I've got a huge constituency with many islands, I suppose my proudest achievement was winning.'

To stand in the same seat twice shows touching dedication and, although it is never as good as an outright victory, there is a certain grim satisfaction to be had in shrinking the size of your opponent's majority bit by bit.

Gwyneth Dunwoody let her name go forward for selection in Exeter, in the early 1960s a safe Conservative seat, 'because I was told by one of the officials of the Labour Party that it was fixed for a friend of mine, which just shows how much you can rely on internal information!' It had never occurred to her that she would actually get the candidacy. 'I then had to go home and explain it to my husband, who was furious of course. But once I get a job I do it, that's one of the hazards.' In 1964 she brought the majority right down, and in 1966 she won.

The Speaker Betty Boothroyd stood for seventeen years in unwinnable seats before she was selected for West Bromwich, and even then she had problems.

'Oh yes, people were quite happy for you to fight a seat they knew you wouldn't win, but it was very good indeed to get a seat that was winnable.

'When I first went to West Bromwich I didn't have the support of some of the women. There was one woman I remember distinctly – she asked me a question and made the comment, "Well I don't think I'm going to vote for you because you're unmarried, you don't know anything about life, you don't have any children or know what it is to make ends meet on a low income. You don't know how to run a house. I'm certainly not going to vote for you." My reply to her was, "Because I don't have those responsibilities I have more time to look after people like you."'

Diana Organ suspects that the West Gloucestershire Labour Party 'looked a bit sideways' at her when they selected her to contest the seat in 1992. 'I was a woman, I was a middle-class woman, I didn't come from the area,' she remembers. 'But on the other hand they were astute enough to say – we think she might work very hard. We think actually we could have a good campaign out of her – and I have to say that we ran an excellent campaign . . . we took what was an 11,000 majority down to 4,900. We shook them about a bit.' The boundaries changed for 1997 and what remained of the old constituency was renamed Forest of Dean. Organ's majority is now a respectable 6,343.

In Rossendale and Darwen, Janet Anderson also took two bites at the cherry, decimating the Conservatives' 9,000 majority in 1987. In 1992 she won the seat by 120 votes. In 1997 the majority rose to a very comfortable 10,949.

Common sense and local opinion often discourage candidates from trying the same seat more than twice. Even so, when Ann Keen lost Brentford and Isleworth a second time in 1992, she was determined to have another go: 'We just lost it by 2,000 votes and, in actual fact, the organisation lost it because there were over 3,000 promised that didn't vote. I have always lived there and I have worked there, I have been a member of local groups and organisations. I just wanted to see it through, and I did – it's a 14,000 majority, which is just incredible.'

Though open to charges of political careerism, free-floating prospective parliamentary candidates (PPCs) often stand a better chance of getting to the House than their local party activist competitors. With no predetermined geographical loyalty to constrict them, they are able to look upon vacant constituency seats with equal affection, and free to chase after every ambitious politician's dream: a safe, winnable seat. This appears to have been particularly true of the eleven Conservative women I spoke to. Nine of them had eagerly put themselves forward for parliamentary selection and seven, when they failed to be elected first time round, went on to brighter, fresher constituencies straight away.

Marion Roe (Conservative, Broxbourne) decided to stand for parliament when she saw the extreme left wing of the Labour Party taking over in the mid-1970s. She rang up Conservative Central Office and made an appointment. It was as simple as that. 'I want to become a Member of Parliament,' she told the official there. 'How do I go about it?' Eleanor Laing was equally single-minded. Failing to win the safe Labour seat of Paisley North in 1987 but still wanting to be in politics full time, she went to work as a special adviser to John MacGregor who had just been made Secretary of State for Education. She stayed with him right through the 1992 campaign and moved on two years later to the Policy Unit at the Institute of Directors. Thus armed, she set about finding herself a safer seat. Theresa May (Conservative, Maidenhead) told me she had 'wanted to be involved in politics and go into parliament for some time . . . a long time'. So had Julie Kirkbride. 'It had always been in the back of my mind.'

Thirty-eight per cent of the 1997 parliament's Conservative women won a seat in their first election; even so Conservative Central Office warns all PPCs that on average it takes twelve years to get to parliament starting from scratch. The key, of course, is getting yourself selected for a safe seat. After coming second six times in selections for safe seats, Roe was elected for Broxbourne in 1983 and made it in eight years. Caroline Spelman (Conservative, Meriden) survived the notorious selection board weekend ('Apparently it's modelled on Sandhurst entry,' she told me, 'it's so tough, after that you can probably get through anything') and was put on the official list in 1989.

She found a candidacy quite easily in 1992, but in 1997 the competition was more fierce. She worked out she had an interview just about every week from October to April, as many as twenty-seven in all. By February it was looking as if she wasn't going to get a seat. So far the Conservative Party had only selected sixty-five women candidates. Although Spelman didn't believe she had been actively discriminated against, it was still very hard to take. 'I wouldn't have given up,' she said, but the thought of having to wait another five years was depressing. 'You have to keep the flame burning.'

Ann Widdecombe (Conservative, Maidstone and The Weald) told me she never let it get her down, but 'when you've had a long round of seats and particularly when you've come second a lot, you do start to wonder are you actually ever going to click?' Only 25 per cent of Conservative women MPs won their first selection, compared with 45 per cent from the Labour Party.

Colne Valley CLP and former Sheffield City councillor Kali Mountford clicked immediately. It was her first selection, and she won it on the very first ballot. To her surprise, Gisela Stuart found her selection process just as easy. Turning up to the first branch meeting in Birmingham Edgbaston, she didn't think she stood a chance of getting the nomination. 'I mean, this was a trial run. I delivered two speeches. I didn't know a single person in the constituency.' Later she asked her supporters why they had voted for her. They told her it was because she answered questions as if she was going to run the country tomorrow. Maria Fyfe decided to have a go for her local constituency, Glasgow, Maryhill, when the incumbent Labour MP retired unexpectedly before the 1987 election. A shortlist of five was drawn up, and in her own words, she 'fell into it'.

Unlike Mountford, Stuart and Fyfe, most of the women I spoke to found selection a truly gruelling experience. Patricia Hewitt remembers trying to get selected for a London seat in 1977, when those on the hard left of the local Party had organised into a highly effective faction. They obviously saw her as a threat, and managed to keep her off the shortlist, even though she had 'this great string of nominations'. Eventually the Electorate Committee agreed to put her back on the shortlist and all the nominees went through to the next stage of the process: the selection conference. When it came to Hewitt's turn to speak, 'One man after another – and it was all men – popped up and asked these staggeringly hostile questions.'

Sometimes sensitivity to criticism and a general lack of confidence can act as a vital spur. The story of Anne Campbell's selection for Cambridge is the hare and the tortoise all over again. She was persuaded to stand by a group of much younger women in her constituency. 'They were all in their twenties, and very keen to have a woman Member of Parliament. I think they just thought I was probably their best bet, so they made a concerted effort to get me there.' Mark Todd (new Labour Member for South Derbyshire), the obvious next in line, had most of the nominations and five applicants went through to the shortlist. 'I was really just determined I wasn't going to do badly,' she remembered. 'You know, I didn't think I was going to beat Mark because there just seemed such an overwhelming preference for him in the nomination process, but I was just determined I was going to give him a good run for his money.' She worked hard on her speech and prepared herself for every question she could anticipate. In the end she beat him by just two votes.

Putting yourself up for your home constituency, you run the risk of treading on the political aspirations of friends and colleagues. Being an outsider, then, has its advantages. Having spent a year and a half nursing the constituency of Staffordshire Moorlands, Charlotte Atkins was selected 'by a pretty overwhelming majority', in preference to the Constituency Chair. She told me it caused a certain amount of bitterness and several local Party officers resigned. 'But in retrospect it was probably quite a good thing, because it meant a clean slate. We had a new team of people who were willing to work along modern lines.'

In the end, however well or little you know the Constituency Labour Party (CLP), the final selection decision still comes down to fellow Party members and, according to Linda Perham, this is what makes the process so tough. 'You've got people in your own Party who are politically knowledgeable asking you about absolutely everything. To put yourself through that you have to have really decided you want to do it, even if it's an unwinnable seat.'

There's a lot to be learnt, of course, from fighting unwinnable seats. Hazel Blears's first candidacy was in Tatton in 1987. 'It was quite good fun, because we knew we wouldn't win and it was excellent training. I think we increased the Labour vote there by 26 per cent, so I had a very good result, and that obviously says to people that you're a good candidate and you know what you're doing.' Fighting Newbury in 1979, Joan Ruddock lost her deposit. 'It was an absolutely vile campaign, because it was the Liberals' second best margin at the time, so horrible things were done to me – impersonations, illegal leaflets, all sorts of things.' In spite of this trial by fire, she caught the bug.

Linda Gilroy came second in a couple of selections for seats in 1992 and ended up standing in South East Cornwall 'which, as I used to say privately at least, if we had won we would have had a one-party state. I mean you would have had to have a bigger majority than we've turned out this time. I sort of served an apprenticeship there, and I enjoyed it.' It can also be seen as a demonstration of Party loyalty. Charlotte Atkins knew she wasn't going to win the Eastbourne by-election in 1990, but thought of it as a job that had to be done. Quite a number of Labour's loyal apprentices were taken by surprise when their so-called unwinnables turned pink on 1 May.

While some of the women I spoke to cheerfully regarded their first candidacy as a training ground, others fought to win. Julia Drown was flattered when people from Oxford and Abingdon West suggested she apply, but knew it was going to be a Liberal Democrat target seat. She phoned Diana Organ, whom she had met through Oxfordshire County Council, for advice. Organ predicted that she would enjoy campaigning, but was very unlikely to win. 'But if you're serious about this, there are all these other seats,' she told her. In the end, Drown was selected to fight South Swindon. 'I don't have a really great sense of humour,' she said, and she didn't see how contesting an unwinnable seat would be a bundle of laughs. 'Whatever I do, I do seriously, so I couldn't do an election campaign just for fun.' Jane Griffiths felt the same. 'I don't want to fight a battle I can't win,' she said.

When Claire Curtis-Thomas was selected by Crosby CLP in

1995 she did not really think she would get into parliament. 'I've come here too early,' she told me. 'I wasn't expecting to be here until I was forty. I've never got involved in anything where I didn't win and, you know, the prospect of having secured the seat which was the hundred and twentieth in the country was pretty depressing, because what it meant was I knew I could win, but it would mean an inordinate amount of hard work.' Not that she was afraid of that. She planned the whole campaign like a military exercise. When Party HQ offered to send over a VIP to boost morale, she told me, she was horrified. 'All that did was throw our canvassing into total disarray. Instead of me knocking on doors and doing things that people appreciate, I had the prospect of swanning around with somebody. I don't think it was even a front-bench spokesman. But whatever, it meant a disruption to our routine.'

The Labour Party's now legendarily efficient election strategy was to concentrate efforts and extra funds in ninety designated key seats. Laura Moffatt, who describes herself as 'the most pessimistic candidate you will ever find', appreciated the extra help, as did the youngest woman MP, Claire Ward (Labour, Watford). 'We were what the Labour Party was calling a Stand Alone Seat.' This meant she had a minimal chance of winning, but because there was a key seat near by, she received a lot of high-profile visits and attention from head office.

Jenny Jones, in Wolverhampton South West, agreed that the strategy was good but did not approve of the way they delivered it. 'I just thought it was demeaning,' she told me. 'Most of us had been councillors, we'd run our own businesses, you know. We didn't pretend we knew it all, but there was an assumption we knew nothing, that we were all idiots. They never bothered to find out what we could do. There was just this blanket [assumption] that none of us knew what we were doing, that none of our CLPs had ever campaigned in the past.'

Like Ward's Watford constituency, South Swindon was a Stand Alone Seat too, something Julia Drown remembers feeling pretty disappointed about at the time. Even so, the regional Party thought they stood a good chance of winning and gave support. Suddenly Drown started to enjoy herself, particularly going round some of the more Conservative areas and hearing lifelong Tories say they were going to vote Labour. 'You walk up these huge drives and you get there and you have this marvellous reward.'

Converging upon Westminster to sign themselves in after what was probably the most hi-tech campaign in British electoral history, new MPs had a foretaste of the chaos that would dominate their lives for the next few months. Gillian Shephard remembers it well. Although they had had six full weeks in which to do it, House of Commons staff were cleaning the cloakroom. Why they had chosen that particular day she couldn't guess. 'You couldn't hang anything up because they were Brasso-ing the pegs,' she sighed. Fortunately the beginning of May was unseasonably warm, but even without the queue for coat-hangers, signing in alone took two whole days. 'I believe in a bit of pomp and all that,' one MP muttered at the time, 'but this is just a joke.'

All the same, Labour's sixty-four new women MPs must have felt incredible in those first few days.

Jane Griffiths: 'I suppose my head was reeling, really. I hadn't expected to win, I thought I was going to but it's not the same as expecting to. In the few days between 1 May and actually arriving here I don't think I'd slept very much and it was very very unreal. I arrived with loads and loads of other people and I just thought, "This can't be me. This can't really be me."'

According to Beverley Hughes, it felt 'like a very powerful historical experience'. Ann Cryer agreed. 'You felt as though you were part of history really.' Maria Eagle 'didn't feel it was real' either. 'I had to be persuaded by my sister to take my car. I was going to go on the bus and, you know, sneak in,' she remembered. 'We all took copies of our election addresses so we could show them to anybody who was dubious about who we were,' though, as half of parliament's first set of twins, this was hardly going to be a problem.

Of course it was very different when Ann Taylor first arrived in 1974. For a start there was less need for security. 'You literally turned up with your suitcase and said "I'm a new Member of Parliament", and they sort of pointed you round to various rooms.'

Laura Moffatt came by Tube. 'I was a complete fool really, because I came out of Westminster station and . . . my eyes filled with tears. I can feel it again when I speak about it.' Ann Keen had been to Westminster plenty of times, visiting her husband, MP for Feltham and Heston, Alan Keen. Arriving as an MP herself, however, was a very different experience. 'I couldn't believe how it affected me, and neither could Alan.' Usually assertive and full of confidence, she suddenly became shy. 'I found myself saying, "Where are you going now? Well, I'll come with you then."' It took two or three weeks for her to get over it.

Labour's new women MPs, of course, had a double victory to celebrate. Not so in 1992, when Tessa Jowell won her seat. She spent the first two weeks walking on air before the bubble burst, she remembers, and she was suddenly hit by 'this sense of awful gloom that everybody else felt, that we hadn't won at all'. In 1997 people were still predicting the Labour Party would never hold power again, and several of the Labour women I spoke to admitted they had shared that pessimism. Last year's landslide made those early May days seem twice as weird and emotional.

As you would expect, most of the 1997 intake had visited the Palace of Westminster before their election and some, like Eleanor Laing, Angela Smith and Lorna Fitzsimons, had worked there as advisers, assistants or lobbyists. Even so, stepping across the worn stone threshold of St Stephen's entrance in their new capacity was, for many, like stepping through the doors of a time machine. 'It was just like medical school in the fifties and early sixties,' remembered Liberal Democrat MP for Richmond Park, Dr Jenny Tonge. 'And some of the Tories, and it is mostly Tory MPs and Ministers, walk around like old-style Health Service consultants. You know, the type you saw in the *Doctor* films. They strut, they have an air of born to rule.'

Melanie Johnson and Jacqui Smith were vividly reminded of their first days at university. 'It's like when you start at Oxford,' Smith, a Hertford College alumna, told a meeting of the Oxford Labour Club. 'Lots of fantastic buildings, lots of people wearing funny clothes. You're surrounded by people who share your interests, but who at the same time are extremely competitive as well, and there is this big buzz of excitement.' Diana Organ agreed. 'It's a real cross between an Oxford college and a girls' boarding school,' she told me. Arriving at Westminster made Geraldine Smith feel like a new girl too. 'I've never been to a public school,' she said, 'but I feel like I'm just beginning my term at one.'

'Some people said it's like joining school,' Caroline Flint (Labour, Don Valley) remembered. 'But it wasn't like any school I went to.' And it wasn't like any school Labour MP for Erewash and former head teacher Liz Blackman ever worked in either. 'The behaviour sometimes is still public-school dormitory stuff. I mean, it really disgusts me.' Particularly in the Chamber. 'Some of the Members putting their feet up on the Dispatch Box – I mean if they'd been on my council they would have been out of the door for doing that.'

Phyllis Starkey was taken even further back in time. 'It was a bit like being at nursery school on the first day,' she said, almost wistfully, 'because you also felt very small.' But if there is something poignant about the thought of these successful, powerful women reduced to a state of childish helplessness and awe by the atmosphere of the Palace, there is something sinister about it too; as if the very walls and fabric of the building conspired to bring out the worst in their new female occupants. After the longest election campaign this century, it was all too much for a tired and emotional Helen Brinton, who threw a tantrum in the Whips' office when she realised how long the wait for a room of her own was going to be. 'They were very controlled,' she said, 'and I did write them a nice note afterwards.'

In Britain, election results take practical effect as soon as they are known. John Major had until noon on 2 May to vacate 10 Downing Street, the first link in a complex chain-reallocation of office space. Rooms are portioned out strictly in accordance with government and parliamentary seniority, so everybody had to wait until Tony had picked his team. Judy Scott Thomson in the Serjeant-at-Arms office worked with government and opposition Whips to fit the rest of the puzzle together as quickly as possible, and the change-over was completed in record time. Even so, for the new women Members at the bottom of the pecking order, four weeks felt like a very long wait. Former Health Service accountant Julia Drown was itching to take control of the whole procedure. She would have charged any defeated Member not out of his or her room by a certain deadline a £10,000 fine, she told me, 'or dustbin bags for everything'.

'For quite a while I was operating off a telephone on a com-mittee corridor, you know, a window-ledge,' Diana Organ said. Maria Eagle had had a similar experience. 'It's absurd, really, and I'm not the only one who thinks so. At the point at which you've just been elected and there is maximum interest in what you're doing and people want you to help them, you're suddenly put into a place where it's almost impossible to respond to requests.' Even with her experience on Westminster Council, Karen Buck had 'no idea of the sheer scale of demand that would fall upon you within twenty-four hours of being elected'. She told me she felt 'like a cork in the ocean'.

As commentators praised the government for having 'hit the ground running', constituency members in their thou-sands took the opportunity to introduce themselves to the new MPs. Maria Eagle had a sack full of post each morning. 'It's delivered to the Post Office in the Member's Lobby and you go and collect it and the longer you don't collect it, the bigger it gets.' Every day Beverley Hughes received 'this huge mountain of letters that would take an hour and a half just to open and put into piles'. It was the same for Tessa Jowell in 1992. 'Like being hit by an avalanche,' she remembers, 'an avalanche of letters.'

Moving from committee corridor window-ledge to an office of one's own may be taken as a sign that things are at last beginning to settle down, but the trials and tribulations of a new MP do not stop there. The House of Commons runs like 659 separate small businesses and how she spends her £47,568 per annum office allowance is left entirely to the Member's discretion. Choosing what computer package to buy is hard enough. Trying to recruit a secretary or assistant presents a whole new order of difficulty. Two hundred economics graduates replied to Ruth Kelly's Monday *Guardian* advertisement. Julie Morgan had 900 applicants for a job in her constituency office in Cardiff North.

And even then, when the equipment has been delivered and your fresh-faced research assistant has peeled it out of its styro-packaging and plugged it in, there is still plenty of scope for disaster. It took two engineers several hours to sort out Jenny Jones's fax. 'I thought it was ever so funny you know, these two men crawling around the floor, lifting carpets, swearing at each other, running downstairs to some bloke who also got sworn at,' she told me. 'And the end result is it isn't a fax line, it's someone else's phone line, so no one can fax me at all now!' For an institution that regards itself as the Mother of Parliaments, communication with the outside world seems remarkably low on the agenda.

Former NUPE research officer Judy Mallaber had not realised the extent of parliamentary isolation: 'You don't watch the TV news any more because you are voting at that time, let alone the other normal programmes that you might watch that other normal people do. Just having time to read the newspapers in the morning – it's very easy to get astonishingly cut off. You could easily get cocooned here, and have quite a comfortable cultural life.'

The Speaker Betty Boothroyd was delighted to make her entrance as an MP after twenty years as a secretary: 'Oh, it was wonderful! Two o'clock in the morning to find when the returning officer gave you the numbers, to find you had won at last after all those years, and of course to come back here.

Now I came as a Member – very different. As secretaries here we were only allowed in some areas of the House and not in its entirety. It felt really grand to come here for the first time as a Member.'

When Marion Roe first arrived, she was lonely. 'My male colleagues would say to me, "Welcome, my dear. Lovely to see you. Now, if there is anything you need to know, don't hesitate to ask" – and then they'd be off down the corridor, and they'd done their bit. And I thought, actually, I don't know what I don't know, so how do I know what I should be asking them?'

Glenda Jackson (Labour, Hampstead and Highgate) agreed. 'I think it's like a great big beehive, actually. I mean the Chamber is the kind of centre of it, and everybody dashes off to their own little cell to get on with their work.' According to Teresa Gorman (Conservative, Billericay), 'The place is a rabbit warren. It certainly takes some exploring.' Joan Humble went further, saying she thought, 'They ought to give us a compass and a ball of string when we first arrive.'

But there is more than physical geography to finding your way around the Palace of Westminster. Other new MPs confessed that what they had been most disorientated by was the invisible labyrinth of obscure conventions and unwritten rules. 'What I can't stand is the fact that you break rules without knowing it,' said former teacher Eileen Gordon (Labour, Romford). 'You only learn what you've done wrong when you've done it.' As Kali Mountford discovered, sitting on the Finance Bill Committee. She was astonished to hear the Committee Chair interrupting an important speech with the fierce announcement, 'Members are allowed to consume water, which we supply, and prescribed medicines only. I know of no medical purpose for a round sweet with a hole in it. You shall desist.' The Member sitting next to her slipped his Polos back into his blazer pocket like a ticked-off schoolboy. In another session, some of the men on the committee were reprimanded for having removed their jackets without permission.

Even though she found the House of Commons 'very, very

seductive', Jane Griffiths felt uncomfortable with 'all the wood panelling and deliberately meaningless words and procedures and things which when someone explains them to you are quite simple'. The place reminded Jenny Jones of a Hollywood film set. She accepted that the pomp and ceremony might once have served a purpose, which 'perhaps the Speaker and her department know', but now it is simply a disguise for the fact that 'actually this place doesn't really work. Underneath it all is chaos.'

Beverley Hughes agreed: 'Unnecessarily opaque, unnecessarily bureaucratic and unnecessarily unconventional. After eleven years in local government I'm used to meetings, I'm used to decision-making in that kind of debating forum. But some of the rules and systems they have here I've not met anywhere else. It just takes a long time to get a handle on them and you feel disempowered and disabled and deskilled.'

In the same way that English Heritage has to be called in to supervise all changes to the physical appearance of the building, so there is also a kind of unofficial, self-appointed committee dedicated to the preservation of quaint tradition. Betty Boothroyd (Speaker, West Bromwich West), is perhaps its most influential member.

Shadow Leader of the House, Gillian Shephard is also a staunch defender. 'I always find it a little unconvincing that people strain every nerve to get selected and to get elected and then, when they get here, the first thing they want to do is change the nature of the very thing they fought to achieve.

'Arriving at the House of Commons takes you one of two ways. You either think, "How very romantic this is, look at the Speaker's Procession, isn't it amazing to start every day with prayers, I adore all this business with the Mace." You either think that, or you think, "Doesn't the Speaker have better things to do than march through the entire palace at two twenty-five every day in robes?" I must say I fall very much into the first category. I think here we have something very special.'

Ann Winterton is another traditionalist: 'Many of the traditions that take place and are part of our daily life have hidden meaning. It's hidden in our history but it's very valid. We do things for a purpose, and I would be very sad if that was all swept away.'

In a way, experienced parliamentarians are like connoisseurs. They have learned to savour the taste of tradition, to feast on historical resonances that incomers cannot even detect. Dare to suggest that the Palace of Westminster is an archaic institution that would be better off turned into a museum, and they will assume you are a philistine.

It took Margaret Hodge two years to understand how to make the House of Commons work to her advantage, and maybe this deliberate, contrived, obscurity is its most 'clubbish' characteristic. Gisela Stuart compared it to learning the rules of chess – mastering them gives one a great sense of achievement. Although, of course, the rules and conventions that inform correct parliamentary behaviour are far more complicated, and most members have to pick them up as they go along; how quickly depends on the individual but, sooner or later, everybody settles in. Former postal worker Geraldine Smith agreed that Westminster was a strange place, but did not feel she had found fitting in particularly difficult. 'I think if I ever start considering it normal I'll start worrying,' she promised, ignoring the fact that by then, of course, it will be too late.

'It's frightening how quickly it becomes your everyday surroundings,' Sandra Osborne (Labour, Ayr) told me. 'I can understand how people get in the system and really stop questioning the outmoded practices because, like everything else in life, you just become used to it.' Anne Begg has resolved to make a list of some of her own criticisms of the way the place is organised, at once. 'If you don't get it down now, you'll soon go native.' Helen Brinton, on the other hand, cannot wait to assimilate. 'I want to feel that I'm a constant player in this place. I don't want to feel like an *arriviste*.'

They coped with it all. An exhausting campaign followed by total confusion when they arrived at Westminster. They sent hand-written letters to constituents from makeshift offices in the corners of committee rooms. They hired secretaries, they bought copiers and fax machines. They perched on windowsills and tried to return phone calls, but had no numbers themselves on which they could be reached. They begged reading lamps and modems from the Serjeant-at-Arms' department, and they did their first experimental negotiations with the Whips. And then they turned their attention to the biggest problem of all – getting to know Westminster man.

3

FACE TO FACE WITH
WESTMINSTER MAN

UNTIL 1997 THE HOUSE of Commons was at least 90 per cent male. The May election almost doubled the number of female MPs; but women are still very much in the minority, and how they get on with the men, how men treat them, and the variations between the way men and women tackle their work have been much talked about since the new session began.

We asked women Members to identify the differences between them and their male colleagues. Lynne Jones argued that the chief male advantage is being 'much better at bull-shitting'. She admitted cheerfully, 'I can't bullshit at all.' For Cheryl Gillan, the key difference concerned attention to detail. 'Women are better at paying attention to detail than men. Men often take a broadbrush view.' Gillian Merron and Jenny Jones agreed that men seem capable of coping with only one task at a time, and need an army of support staff to help them just do that.

The Housing Minister, Hilary Armstrong, thought the differences were obvious from the start: 'Very often the men who come here have relied on their mothers and their wives to sort their daily life out. And they arrive here and they don't know how to sort the day out. They don't know how to prepare for the day, other people have done that for them. The women, it doesn't matter what background you come from, that's not what your life has been like.'

Rosie Winterton said she thought women spent a lot of their time soothing people down, as opposed to winding them up – which she saw as a male skill.

This picture of men as ill-organised dissemblers who can only deal with one subject at a time and need a team of supporters to run their daily lives may be extreme, but it was asserted over and over again with confidence by women Members.

Ex-Conservative Minister Ann Widdecombe, on the other hand, strongly disagreed: 'I think there's far too much whingeing and whining going on on the part of women. When I first came in, everyone was saying "Oh isn't it dreadful, there's only 45 of us and 600 of them." I have no doubt that if you are a woman in this place, you have a huge advantage. There are still comparatively few – both major parties want to promote women. If you are any good, you'll get on, you're effectively competing with other women so you're competing in a much smaller pool than your male colleagues. My consistent experience has been that if I want a bad time, I look to women for it. When I was going through selection committees, if I went into a room and most of the people in the room were women, I wrote the seat off before I started. Similarly, when I was going through the handcuffing of women debate, the Labour men were all perfectly reasonable. The Labour women were absolutely ghastly. The idea that women civilise the House is wrong. Some of the greatest hecklers in this place are women.'

Most female MPs felt that one of the key differences between them and their male colleagues was that men would always put themselves forward, but that women were mostly shy violets who did not want to volunteer unless they were almost overqualified for the job.

Cheryl Gillan: 'If you put down ten necessary criteria for a job specification, the woman will read it, and if she's got eight of the requirements and two are missing, she won't apply for the job, whereas the man might only have six of the ten things required and he'll still apply anyway.'

Maria Eagle: 'Women are much more concerned to present themselves properly. Women won't present themselves for a job unless they can do almost everything that's required to do it. Men will go for something beyond what they can do and grow into it.'

Joan Ruddock thought that conscientiousness was a more common trait amongst women, whereas Jane Griffiths and Charlotte Atkins both cited lack of confidence tinged with pragmatism as the defining characteristics of women in the House. According to Atkins, if women 'don't think there's much chance of getting themselves elected, they don't put themselves forward. Simple as that. Very task-orientated.' Anne Begg also felt that girls were simply not brought up to push themselves forward, whereas boys were.

Hazel Blears, who spent a lot of time visiting schools and youth groups while she was a candidate, confirmed these views, pointing out that boys were more ambitious right from the start, and across the board: 'Some of the aspirations young women have are so low. They all want to be beauty therapists or work with children. You don't find one aspirant marine biologist amongst the lot. We can do something in raising the aspirations of young women, particularly from working-class communities – to say there are a whole range of possibilities out there. You can do it too. We have a responsibility to do that.'

And Gwyneth Dunwoody observed that men and women approached problems in different ways. 'A man given an inadequate budget will say to his directors, I can't operate on that. You must increase the budget. Give me more staff. A woman given an inadequate budget goes away and tries to do it all. It's a fundamental difference.'

Candy Atherton said she thought it was still up to women to doubly prove themselves and Jacqui Smith believed that, as far as Westminster was concerned, the biggest problem for women was still simply getting there. But once women become MPs, it is clear that those strong differences do not fade.

Teresa Gorman: 'Men nearly always come in with some connections. The same regiment. The same school. The same profession. They play the same sport. They're all points at which they can touch other people, but women don't have that. I don't think women network in the way men do. Men by nature think of coteries which preclude women, so you do feel awfully lonely. No one tells you how to behave, so you tend to be yourself. You end up on the front page of the papers for saying what you feel and with, apparently, a big question mark over your ability to act as a team player. That's what men are – team players. All team players. They tell you that loyalty is more important than anything else, including intellect and experience.'

Marion Roe: 'Men love to operate in gangs. It's just like the school playground. The majority of boys will be in gangs. There'll be a leader and his lieutenant, and they'll all be working in a gang. Girls tend to have a best friend.'

Jane Griffiths thought men deliberately complicated things and used language which was hard to understand. 'When they have train sets, little boys like to have technical names for everything. They can't just say it's a wheel, it has to be a so-and-so gauge something-or-other. I think it's something in the Y chromosome and it very much permeates this place.'

Two Cabinet Ministers with experience of male and female Members working in their teams also highlighted the fundamental differences between the way women and men do things. Ann Taylor, the Leader of the House, is the Chair of the Modernisation Committee. 'Women still get fed up more quickly at the silliness and the pettiness and the ya boo. The common-sense approach is quite clearly there, more evident with women. Our life experience is such that we're more attuned to trying to sort things out. I think there's a greater tendency in blokes to bluff it out when they don't know – afraid to admit they don't know something. I think women are more likely to ask why or why not.'

The President of the Board of Trade, Margaret Beckett (Labour, Derby South), went further: 'There's a tendency with women – if you say no, you can't do that, don't do that, etc. and they don't agree or don't see why, then they ask why not. And if you say because those are the rules, women will say, "Well, the rules are stupid", or, "They ought to be changed." They want a reason. On the whole if you say to a man that those are just the rules, they'll say OK.'

The Conservative Party's most senior woman politician Gillian Shephard said that she hoped that now that one in five Members were female, changes might happen in her own Party. 'Our Party is very imbued with public school and Oxbridge and all that – "That's how it is old boy, that's how we do things."' She felt strongly that women on the whole will not tolerate that sort of attitude. 'They've been broken open by having families, and they've had to grind away in unconventional manners to get here and so they're very impatient with "We've always done it this way."'

Anne Campbell felt that women, by virtue of being a conspicuous element in the House, had to try much harder, and endure harsher criticism. 'Men are just much more invisible in this place. They can get away with more.'

In her book *The Bastards*, Teresa Gorman talked about the way she was treated by men outside her group who wanted her to vote with the government. Once she was sandwiched between two hostile members in the chamber:

One said something like, 'You know she's talking about voting against the government?' The other one said, 'I always said we shouldn't let women in here in the first place. They're a thundering nuisance.'

I realised they were trying to provoke me, but it was bait I wasn't going to rise to. The first said, 'A woman's place is in the home.'

'Yes, flat on her back.'

I felt trapped. I didn't want to get up and leave. Why should I? On the other hand, I didn't want to just sit there as if I didn't mind . . .

One of them said, 'Do you think Teresa would be any good on her back? I wonder what kind of knickers she wears . . .'

I could no longer put up with it. I exploded. 'Why don't you go somewhere else and find someone else to talk dirty to if you feel like that?'

'I thought you'd be enjoying it. I thought that was what

you liked about this place. Plenty of men.'

'A few men treat you as a colleague, an equal. Most men, particularly, I found, in the Conservative Party are stuck in the 1930s . . .

'I am not one of those women who feel I must go about my business aggressively and I do rather tend to butter them up. There are things as a woman which you can do which help to break down the barriers for the men. I've found that colleagues of mine, after they have known me vaguely for a year, or perhaps five years, they'll say, "I'm really surprised to find Gorman has a brain as well as a body."

'Desmond Morris wrote a marvellous book called *Man Watching*. He recommended breaking down the physical barrier. So when they were being exceptionally patronising, I would tap them on the arm or squeeze them on the arm which a woman can do, but a man can't and say, "You don't really mean that do you? You are being silly." And immediately they begin to sort of melt. If they are really stuffy, I tap them on the nose, which is absolutely brilliant, it's like melting a block of ice. Ambience is very important. You don't antagonise them. Some of the men strongly antagonise some of the women.'

Edwina Currie: 'When I got to Westminster, I found myself with a range of people the like of which I had never seen before and I realised how wise my decision had been not to try for seats in the south of England and the Shire Counties, where one breadwinner earns enough and there's no necessity for anyone else to go to work, where women were seen in a different role, essentially as handmaidens. Most of my male colleagues in the Tory Party had non-working wives so I was a kind of aberration, and they clearly thought I was a bit odd. One or two of them tested the water to see whether I'd come looking for a man, because of course women don't function without men, you see. So they tried it on a bit. One or two tried it on quite blatantly. I don't think I actually slapped anyone's face but I got fairly close.

'I was furious – I got elected the same way as they did. I'm better educated, better qualified than the lot of them. It did annoy me and it made me more ambitious to do well, which probably annoyed them even more.'

Barbara Castle was a Labour Cabinet Minister, off and on, between 1964 and 1976. I asked her what part sex played when woman got to the top. Were there sexual undertones in her relationship with the Prime Minister?

'I was very close to Harold politically. I didn't feel about him . . . particularly sexy. What I liked about him – he was the cheeky chappy of politics. He had a brilliant brain, and of course I hate pomposity in politicians more than anything. He never practised it, and I never treated him as a prickly PM who had to be dealt with with reverence. I used to cheek him back. Every time he started rolling off statistics at me, I used to start quoting poetry back at him, which used to silence him and we had that good matey relationship and political affinity.'

Barbara Castle enjoyed being a woman surrounded by powerful men. 'I'm a very feminine person by instinct. I always like to look my best. I think it's the duty of women, when they're in public life, to cheer up the scene to the best of their ability.'

So did she ever use her attractiveness to exert her power over men? 'I have no great confidence in my sexual attractiveness at all. I used to find it rather amusing, whether in make-up or dress or whatever, to hide my physical disabilities. That's part of the fun. I used to feel better myself if I was well groomed and wearing a pretty dress. Oh, I cared about that very much. I have never been a hair-shirt socialist. I have never been a blue-stocking woman. I owe a lot of my happiness to the fact that I had a husband who perfectly understood that I was going to have a career. He was never jealous of me. He wanted to get into parliament but he used to identify himself so warmly, so generously, with my success.'

But one story she told me revealed that, even if she was charmingly modest about her attractions, her colleagues thought otherwise. Just recently in the House of Lords, she had got chatting with an old workmate. 'There was one laddie there who'd been my Parliamentary Secretary, I think when I was at Social Services, very nice chap. We were talking and I said to him was I an awful boss to work for? "Oh no," he said, "I used to admire the way you handled your Civil Servants. You were very firm but you used sex appeal."

'I said, "But I haven't got any sex appeal you know," and he said very quietly, "You were oozing sex appeal at every pore."

'Now I was totally unaware of that. I haven't any great faith in my physical attractiveness. My model woman would be Pola Negri, tall, slim, with dark hair reclining on a tiger skin, and here I was short, freckled, ginger-haired. I used to suffer acne so I never really believed any man would ever love me for years. I have never been a *femme fatale*. But I think one can have – you watch Margaret Thatcher, that's what she did – a woman can have a very satisfying sexual relationship with one of her entourage without it ever coming to anything. If you are a woman in charge, you've got a retinue of young men whose duty it is to provide your every need. You're a bit like the Queen. You never carry your own money. You never buy your own ticket.'

Teresa Gorman also thought that Margaret Thatcher's sexuality was often easy to spot. 'She flirted outrageously with some of the men. I am sure if you looked at her behaviour in the lobby when some of the men who were part of her inner circle, the Tebbits, the Parkinsons were with her, her manner and body language were quite different.

'She was quite clearly besotted by Gorbachev. And when he came over, she looked twenty years younger. Her hair looked brighter and different and her eyes sparkled. I remember the day when he came to the Commons, he came to speak to Parliament. She was incredible. Almost girlish. She was undoubtedly enormously physically attracted to him and she called him, "A man with whom I could do business."'

Gwyneth Dunwoody: 'Some of the best relationships have been between MPs and MPs. My own experience of politicians – most of them have promised more than they can perform. I think some of them like the odd pint more than they like anything else. But you can't have 600 people, plus all the people who are here who aren't MPs, which comes to thousands, and not have every combination of sexual relationship. Still, the majority are rather boring and staid and stick to their wives.'

Peter and Virginia Bottomley and Nicholas and Ann Winterton, the famous Tory MP couples, have now been joined by Rhodri (Labour, Cardiff West) and Julie Morgan and Alan and Ann Keen on the Labour benches. Bridget and Gordon Prentice (Labour, Pendle) became Members together in 1992 but have now separated. And Andrew Mackay (Bracknell) the Conservative Northern Ireland spokesman and Julie Kirkbride became the first ever couple to marry while they were both Members.

Julie Kirkbride: 'It's a very wonderful thing that's happened to me in the last few months. One of the great pieces of good fortune is that he is a Member for a seat which isn't too impossible. If he had been a Scottish MP it would have made life very hard. It would have meant that the time we had to see one another would have been much reduced. As it is, we both head out west, him on the M4, and me on the M40.'

She went on to explain that of course both of them would put their constituents first at all times: 'but maybe when we are not needed in our own, it would be nice to be together in each other's.'

120 women have arrived at Westminster at a time of other great changes. There were 260 new Members altogether, 40 per cent of the House of Commons, a post-war record. There are bound to be changes, too, in the way men and women get on together.

'Hi, Kev! I was just coming to see you. OK, darling.' The Secretary of State for Northern Ireland turned to me. 'I must stop calling my Private Secretary "darling",' she said. 'He quite likes it, but others don't.'

Mo Mowlam is as friendly and outgoing a Cabinet Minister as there has ever been. She carries the serious responsibility of her position, as Secretary of State for Northern Ireland, lightly. Barbara Castle may have oozed sex appeal, Mowlam oozes warmth, friendliness and power too: a perfect role model for aspiring women politicians. When we finished our interview in the Northern Ireland Office, she did not merely take me to the door of her room, but the front door of the building, where she hugged me goodbye with enthusiasm. She gave the impression of being a woman who is comfortable in her difficult job.

Ann Widdecombe said she enjoyed the House of Commons, too. If it is a man's club, she said, then it is nevertheless a 'very jolly club'. 'I feel part of it,' she continued, 'and not conscious of being a woman.' I asked her about her row with the previous Home Secretary, Michael Howard (Conservative, Folkestone and Hythe) over her support for the prisons boss Derek Lewis, whom Howard had sacked. Did the fact that he was male and she was female have anything to do with it? She thought not. The female slant on the affair, for her, simply emerged from journalistic speculation over her real attitude to Mr Lewis. The media world, it seems, is unable to accept that a woman can respect a man without being romantically or sexually attracted to him. 'I was impressed by Mr Lewis, I was not seduced by him.'

I suggested that it was her male colleagues who were putting it about that she had rather fallen for Derek Lewis, or had a crush on him. She refused to lay the blame at anyone's door, and very reasonably pointed out that the same slights are routinely dealt out to, and endured by, men. 'If a man is promoting a woman, you often get a lot of catty talk that he is actually secretly attracted to her.'

Barbara Castle had a warning message for the new women at Westminster. She pointed out that most of these women were now doing at least two jobs, running homes and families and being Members of Parliament. Realistically, she said, she felt it was unlikely that their husbands were going to 'fully help them' but the women must be careful to make sure they didn't leave their men trailing behind. 'The man must keep his self-esteem,' she said. 'That's very important and the wife's preoccupation should be as much with his self-esteem as hers.'

I thought that perhaps that told us more about Barbara

Castle's marriage than it did about today's female MPs, until a Whip mentioned to me that Barbara and Ken Follett had found their relationship under strain since Barbara became an MP. When I asked Barbara (Labour, Stevenage) about it, she said she had overheard her husband on the phone telling someone that he'd gone to bed alone on more evenings since she had become an MP than in the whole of the last thirty years. And rectifying the problem is not easy. The Folletts had, for instance, booked to go to the opera for Ken's birthday, but even though Labour had a huge majority, the Whips would not let Barbara off for the evening. Barbara said she felt this had nothing to do with her gender, but rather provided evidence of the ridiculous strains which Westminster puts on family life.

There was a victory celebration for Labour women in Brighton. Hundreds crammed into the Claremont Suite at the Metropole Hotel and embraced each other enthusiastically. The stars were out. Mo Mowlam moved round the room in a constant hug of women. Hilary Armstrong, Joan Ruddock, Harriet Harman (Camberwell and Peckham) and Angela Eagle were fêted by female supporters. Plenty of the new girls turned up too. Shona McIsaac brought her husband. She pointed him out to me in a far corner talking to another man. 'Bless him,' said Shona, 'I've lost count of the number of times when I've been one of the few females in a room, and now he's one of two men and he's bonding with the other one!'

Whispers soon began to spread that Tony himself would make an appearance. This was quickly confirmed when the Labour Party Women's Officer Meg Russell gave me a big New Labour smile and said, 'Tony has asked me to ask you (imagine!) not to film what he has to say. It's an informal occasion. He wants to have a private chat with all the women.' I was intrigued. What could he possibly want to say?

Tony was thrust into the room, Cherie at his side. He climbed up on the podium. She stayed on the floor grinning bravely. Much cheering. Hilary Armstrong apologised for Tony in advance. He had a terrible cold and was suffering.

Little sighs of sympathy rose from women here and there. Thinking he had the measure of the meeting, Tony seized his opportunity and with streaming eyes and a sniff announced daringly, 'I know I've come to the right place for a bit of sympathy!' There was a shocked hush, and then, quite strongly, booing and hissing from the women. In his first ten seconds, Tony had managed to get it wrong. Beseechingly, he raised his hands. 'Look. I'll start over again.' There was good-humoured laughter from the women, who like women everywhere, had already forgiven him. But it was a warning. Don't under-rate us. There's a lot of us, and we want changes. Some of us are tired of the way men run things.

So Tony talked about the women themselves – the first time I had heard him do this. At the Labour women's training conference in Bournemouth, he avoided mentioning women at all, and treated the whole event as a mini-Party conference, just another media opportunity. He said that the Chamber was beginning to look a bit more like the world outside. And then he acknowledged that the greatest change of all at Westminster since 1 May had been the arrival of the women themselves. Enthusiastic cheers all round. Blair allowed the possibility that women might change the way things are done and referred back to his first Question Time when he arrived in the Chamber, and the waiting women did what came naturally and clapped.

Clapping is one of those things that simply is not done at Westminster. The slapping of order papers on the bench in front? That's fine. The stamping of feet? Perfectly acceptable, as are a few baritone rounds of 'Hear! Hear!' But no one had ever clapped before. This was a first. We knew the women had arrived. And now we know that Tony knew it too.

The 120 women are part of a much-changed parliament. It feels younger. On 2 May there were ten New Labour MPs aged under thirty. It's a more female House. And it is much less experienced. Forty per cent of Members are first-timers. This was the biggest change in the composition of parliament since 1945.

The Chamber is the tip of the Westminster iceberg, the

visible part of an MP's work. It is the only place where we can watch Ministers and backbenchers. But the importance it plays in the day-to-day life of Members is shrinking. Oratory is no longer a key attribute of stars in the ascendant, but what happens in the Chamber is still the only visible measure of an MP's progress and is much discussed inside and outside the House.

As the Conservative Party conference began in Blackpool, the London *Evening Standard* gave its front page to a story about behaviour in the Chamber. It claimed that the Labour Party were assembling a secret dossier of Tories said to have been chanting sexual abuse at the new intake of women MPs. The *Standard* painted a picture of Labour Whips bent over editing machines late into the night, trying to identify the guilty men on video. The story made the national tabloids and the Radio 4 *Today* programme, but soon petered out for lack of hard evidence. High Tory harassers know better than to get caught on tape, and there is a feeling among long-serving women members that things are not as bad as they used to be. Maria Fyfe believes that televising the House has meant big changes in the way people behave in the Chamber.

'Before the House was televised, the behaviour of a number of MPs late at night was really abominable. They would come in, obviously having wined and dined rather well [*Author's note*: the convention in parliament is that you can never say someone is drunk when they obviously are] and they were grossly offensive. They were making all sorts of sarky remarks to people and trying to put them off their stride, and especially they tried to have a go at the new women who were just in. If she was hesitant in manner, they would seize on that like hounds after a fox.'

Clare Short is enthusiastic about the Chamber: 'There are moments when it's the biggest megaphone in the world and you can get up and say your thing – it's a way of getting the truth out.' But there are times when she too feels that men make it tough for female Members.

'When you make a point of order in a division you have to put this top hat on and be sitting down and one night I did. I came back from dinner and they were in a boozy mood and it must have made them feel a bit cabaretish and they reacted.

'Another time I wore a black jacket with a little kind of bow thing or a tie, and I was on the front bench. They treated me like a woman who's performing for them. There's me and my politics and suddenly they turn it into a game, a parade. As if women are abnormal and they shouldn't be there – and if they are, they're a subject of entertainment.'

She also pointed out some men's inability to cope with female medical matters:

There were a lot of arguments about cervical cancer screening when we didn't have a screening system, and a lot of them would giggle if you mentioned things like that. Very kind of public schoolboy primitive. If there was anything remotely to do with women and their health or the breasts of women, that finished them off completely.'

Ray Michie said that some of the men were bullies who tried to put people off when they were speaking or asking questions. They would be very arrogant and very snide. But she thought that the arrival of so many women would cause habits to change, simply because women would not put up with that kind of nonsense when there was a big group of them.

Jean Corston felt that many of the trouble-makers had gone at the May election. 'There are so few now of those sort of Tory gents who felt the world was made for them and who clearly lived a life of patronage and privilege. It used to enrage me. Their idea of a good day appeared to be being somewhere else for the day, as a director of a company or running a business or whatever and coming in late in the afternoon, having a vote or two, having a good dinner and a bottle of claret, vote at ten o'clock and go home. I felt as though the rest of us ran the place. We put down the questions, we contributed to the debates and the rest of it and I felt those people were completely and absolutely divorced from reality and the electorate. The electorate agreed with me because they turfed them out.'

Mo Mowlam has seen a change already: 'Attitudes of MPs

I thought would never shift, have shifted. Men I would never see, I see acting as human beings. I go in and I see some of the old guys sitting talking to women whom, historically, they would never meet.'

Anne Campbell agrees. 'There's a different atmosphere, there's a different environment. It's an atmosphere that I feel much more comfortable with now than I did then. Even just speaking in the Chamber. You felt previously there was a sort of underlying hostility which was quite intimidating to women. There was a lot of ya boo. The Conservatives hadn't expected to win the last election and they did and they were quite triumphant about it. It was a curious atmosphere and the place wasn't comfortable.'

Margaret Beckett said it was twenty-three years since she was first elected and the biggest single change has been in the number of women Members and the change that had made in the atmosphere of the House. 'There have been other changes in the opposite direction,' she told me. 'The House has become more confrontational and less collegiate and less open in the sense of taking other points of view, which I am afraid all started under Margaret Thatcher. I'm hoping it's something that might begin to change now.'

Glenda Jackson agreed that the sheer number of women makes a difference. 'You see children here, which is marvellous. The overwhelming change is just that there are so many Members of the Labour Party. We have this enormous majority and I think there is a difference in atmosphere. There's an age difference as well. It seems a much younger parliament – which is good.'

Hilary Armstrong, like Tony Blair, feels that the increased numbers of women in parliament merely echo the changes taking place in the wider society; a sign that perhaps Westminster is at last in tune with the mood of the nation.

When Scottish Nationalist Margaret Ewing first came in, there were twenty-seven women Members. She too thinks changes are apparent. 'Helene Hayman, Ann Taylor, Margaret Beckett and I are the survivors of the 1974 intake. We were all young females. The *Guardian* was doing the sexiest MP of the year and that kind of rubbish. I won it the first year. It just wouldn't be politically correct now. Helene said, "They either pat you on the head or pat you on the bottom." The age definition of the house has changed. There's a generation of male MPs who don't expect women to be basically pregnant, in the kitchen or the bedroom. A lot of them are married to women who have careers themselves. Look at Tony Blair. He's not expecting Cherie to give up being a barrister because he happens to be Prime Minister. No more than I would expect my husband to give up his career as a solicitor just because he happens to be my husband. I think that young generation of men has altered it away from the Bufton Tuftons.'

I asked Ann Clwyd (Labour, Cynon Valley) if she thought victories in the on-going fight to feminise Westminster had already been won. 'It's taken me thirteen years to get rid of the male barber here,' she said. But what about more serious reforms? 'That is serious actually. If women have fought hard to get here, then we should have equal treatment when we are here. And in some ways it's more important to have a women's hairdresser than a barber.' Stephen Silverne had been trimming the silver locks of men in grey suits since 1970. When the Serjeant-at-Arms' office hinted that it was time to leave, he complained to the press of discrimination on grounds of political correctness. 'All this sexist stuff is a load of nonsense.'

Clwyd maintains that the same services should be offered to men and women alike. 'You know – women's hair on television – if it's a mess, someone's bound to comment on it. They won't remember what you've said, but they'll remember whether your hair's a mess.' The Serjeant-at-Arms' office put an advert in the *Evening Standard*, provoking enquiries from more than forty hopeful salons. Silverne accepted early retirement. A House of Commons contact has fixed him up with a new job at the Army & Navy Club in Pall Mall.

Joan Walley, who is a leading campaigner for change and modernisation at Westminster, said that the food provided for Members was another area that needed bitter battles to achieve tiny changes. All the food served 'was comfort food', standard tea-room provender being 'beans on toast, egg and bacon, no salad.' Her three-year battle with the Refreshments Director and the Director of Catering is showing signs of success. As the Speaker, Betty Boothroyd, conceded: 'We looked at the menus, the refreshment departments. Women don't necessarily want the same sort of food that men might want.'

But there are also signs that men might be fighting back. The new Chair of the Services Committee is Dennis Turner, the MP for Wolverhampton South East, described by his colleagues as a fifteen-stone Black Country trencherman. Joe Ashton, the sixty-four-year-old MP for Bassetlaw – who is so old-style that he forbade his wife Maggie to be interviewed for this book, on the rather thin grounds that he might write a similar book himself one day – says that it was a coup to get Dennis elected chairman. Joe describes the food as like a Kensington wine bar: 'three lettuce leaves scattered with a spoonful of grated tuna'.

The great canteen war begins to look like another attempt by the media to puff up the Commons war between the sexes. A recent menu in the cafeteria offered broccoli and stilton soup (30p), poached mackerel fillet with tomato and dill sauce (£1.25) and roast striploin of beef with yorkshire pudding (£2.75), which would seem to satisfy both sides. Not a piece of grated tuna in sight.

Many of the new women MPs see Westminster as an old-style gentlemen's club, which they are eager to change. Ruth Kelly summed up their position: 'It's based on the nineteenth-century tradition of men working during the day and going in after work and using it as a club. Going for dinner and then going for a vote after.'

Virginia Bottomley, free now to speak her own mind from the backbenches, was convinced that men were still the winners at Westminster. 'It's all Blair, Brown, Mandelson and Powell, and the girls are given the junior jobs. Women are patronised here. Yesterday I heard a very senior Labour Chairman of a Select Committee introducing the new Member for Watford, saying how young and attractive she looked and I rebuked him. There's a macho culture, but I don't think women should be too self-pitying because it's also a system which works for women.'

I asked the Office Keeper in the Serjeant-at-Arms' office, Jill Pay, what difference she thought the women MPs made to Westminster, and she told me they were much prettier than their male colleagues. They'd brightened the place up with their colourful clothes.

How they looked and what other people thought of their clothes, their hair, their make-up and their figures was to be a big issue for Westminster women over the first few months of the new parliament. But while some loathed every mention of skirt lengths, every count of trousers in the Chamber (women only of course!), others had makeovers and style challenges, relishing every minute of their new visibility.

4

POWER SUITS

IN ELECTIONS THROUGH the 1980s and 1990s, the Labour losers suffered image problems which stayed to haunt them. Michael Foot's famous appearance at the Cenotaph in a donkey jacket was constantly referred to during the disastrous 1983 campaign. By 1997 Labour reckoned it had all that sorted. Male candidates looked pleasant, safe, reliable. They were young to middle-aged, greying to grey. Dark suits by Marks & Spencer, Principles and Next. Sober shirts in white or blue. Silk ties discreetly patterned like the foil wrapping in a better box of chocolates, modern 'eyewear' and conservative haircuts. Acceptable in any High Street as a bank or building society manager, Lion or Round Tabler. Gone for ever were donkey jackets, slacks, sports coats and TUC ties. Goodbye, Mr Byrite.

But what to do with the women? Everyone at Millbank knew that women could be difficult, capable, on a bad campaign day, of appearing in an ocelot mini-skirt or lycra leggings after one unsupervised lunch-hour cheering themselves up at the shops. Labour wanted their women to look as safe as the men. Rules and regulations concerning appearance were faxed from Millbank to female candidates throughout the campaign. Every time I saw Shona McIsaac, she reported the latest diktat. Hair must be tied back neatly. Jangly earrings must be avoided. Restrict decoration to one single piece of 'important' jewellery on the lapel of a suit. Look serious. Look like you mean business.

On the last day of the campaign, John Prescott arrived in

64

Cleethorpes by helicopter for the final push. It was a hot afternoon. His dark suit was very, very serious – so severe it could
probably have come on its own. Shona greeted him in the
middle of a school sports field in a rose pink business suit.
Hair up. Glasses on. Brooch sensible. New Labour – new
image. The crowds cheered this vision of small-town
respectability, and you knew that from tomorrow things
would never be the same.

The new women arrived for the first day of the new term,
women of all ages from all over Britain, trying their best to
look their best on a most important day. The old hands wore
tried and tested outfits that had worked well in the past. The
new girls, battle-scarred foot soldiers weary from a six-week
war, had either splurged on a demob suit (reckoning the bank
manager was good for one more hike in the overdraft) or were
cheerful in freshly Sketchley-ed campaign gear. The Labour
women were asked to gather for a celebratory photo with the
Leader. The next morning the *Daily Mail* published the result
in its now famous supplement, 'BLAIR'S BABES' – THE PROOF
THAT WOMEN REALLY HAVE ARRIVED AT WESTMINSTER.

'The women frothed out of Church House, Westminster in
a multi-coloured tide. It was like Chelsea Flower Show meets
the Girl Guides as the fuschia suits loved by the likes of
Margaret Beckett and Barbara Follett's glittering emerald
green mingled with the more sombre browns and beiges.' So
wrote Bill Mouland, unleashing a tide of fashion comment
which was to infuriate the women, who had been struggling
for months to follow the careful advice of the style gurus at
the Millbank Tower.

Ann Widdecombe seemed at first to have scant sympathy.
'I think Blair's Babes asked for it because they made such a
hoo ha about being women.' However, she admits that 'this
doesn't happen when they [the press] are looking at men . . .
they concentrate much more on ability and achievement and
all the rest of it. I hate to say it but some of the greatest offend-
ers are women journalists.'

Jane Shilling, who writes a style column in *The Times*,
launched a cruise missile the following week:

Who will save Labour's idealistic, visionary and utterly dowdy class of '97 from years of brightly coloured polyester?

All got up for the occasion in what are presumably their best outfits, the female arm of the Labour Party looks like nothing so much as an exceptionally nasty example of municipal planting. Margaret Beckett in shrieking geranium pink, Ann Taylor in blinding lobelia blue, Linda Perham in cruel French marigold orange, and Patricia Hewitt in a jacket covered in writhing herbiage of a kind usually heralded by a sign reading 'Britain in Bloom, runner up, 1997'.

Each and every female MP was appalled. They united in condemnation of this unprovoked assault. One G. Shephard (Mrs) of Norfolk, at home in bed with the flu, rushed in with a defence of her sisters on the green benches opposite. *The Times* didn't realise this was the Conservative Party's most senior female politician, the Rt Hon. Gillian Shephard, MP.

'I wrote to *The Times*, they didn't print it of course. I wrote and said did Jane Shilling know that these women had just come off six weeks' campaigning? Did she know that they would have had to queue up to comb their hair, because there aren't even enough lavatories? Did she know that they were working an eighteen-hour day and polyester is quite handy in those circumstances? Did she know that they were earning less than their French counterparts and less than Cherie Blair and therefore obliged into polyester? I never read anything so infuriating. How could she do that to other women?'

Joan Walley also felt aggrieved by the Shilling piece. Particularly the comment about synthetic fibres. 'What's that got to do with a woman's ability to do her job? I just found it such an undermining article. An offensive article actually.'

Linda Perham: 'The first day I had no idea we were going to have a photo-call of all women MPs and I wore my green trouser suit and my orange blouse, which I thought looked quite nice and *The Times* referred to it as a cruel French marigold colour.

'*The Mail* came up and said why have you got those particular clothes on, and I said I'm wearing a trouser suit and flat
shoes because I have to do a lot of walking round. There is so
much walking round that I wear clothes to be comfortable as
well as what looks good.'

Jane Shilling railed on:

> their terrible shoes, their skirts brutally terminated at mid-
> calf or bang on the kneecap, their ill-cut jackets, every
> single shoulder pad an inch too wide, the result no doubt of
> the baleful influence of Barbara Follett, she of the bile green
> two-piece and criminally matching court shoes . . . Why
> does the team photograph of Mr Blair's new girls so eerily
> resemble a convention of successful Avon Ladies? Did their
> constituencies make them swear on oath on pain of dese-
> lection to wear nothing but ill-fitting polyester two-pieces?

The MPs defended themselves, stoutly pointing out that
they wanted to look businesslike and serious.

Anne McGuire (Labour, Stirling): 'My job in Scotland
meant that I needed to be smart. I actually had the foundation
of a reasonable political wardrobe. What I have had to do
coming down to London is to buy cooler clothes. We could-
n't get over how warm and humid it was. You know you've
constantly got to remember that you could be yanked in to do
a TV interview, which I have been you know, not prepared
for it, so it's all the wee tricks of the trade, like make sure
you've got make-up and all sorts of perfume. I shouldn't say
that, should I?'

Diana Organ: 'We are not over-dressed and power-dressed,
you don't see us looking like something out of Dallas. We
don't go for quite that Margaret Thatcher look, but most of
us have got that happy medium of looking smart and presentable, fairly conventionally dressed while actually reasonably relaxed.

'I went to one parliamentary selection – it was a hot summer's evening and I turned up in a T-shirt and a skirt and Judy
Church was there and she said to me, "Diana, wear a jacket,"

and I said, "Really Judith!" and she said, "Wear a jacket. Because men are funny, you know, you look too much like you are going for a picnic."'

Patricia Hewitt: 'When I started work as a young thing at the National Council for Civil Liberties, I used to wear jeans and sort of trendy jackets, but I didn't exactly look television friendly, and then I did some television training and I thought well, I'm there on television representing the NCCL and I don't want the viewers thinking, "What's she doing wearing jeans on television?" I want them actually listening to what I'm saying.

'As a Member of Parliament, it's a particularly interesting balance, because it's not appropriate to go around looking overdressed. Some of the Tories look as if they're at cocktail parties when they're in the House of Commons.

'I feel that people have a very strong sense that they want their MP to look proper. Neil Kinnock used to say this. He was contemptuous of people like Jeremy Corbyn, who was dressing down and slopping round the place. If you come from a working-class background as Neil does, you would know that basically if you are an MP, you wear your Sunday best every day of the week. He was a great one for properly shining shoes and I think that's right. I think you're expected to look smart.'

Julia Drown admitted that looking smart was important, in some respects an extra, but unspoken duty for an MP. The problem was how to balance that with all the other demands on her. 'I probably do need to go shoe shopping and clothes shopping, but I haven't had time. I'd just like to be completely comfortable and walk around in leggings and do my work in leggings but I can't.'

Phyllis Starkey used to work as a research scientist, and was used to wearing standard laboratory couture: sweaters and jeans. 'I wouldn't dream of dressing in that fashion as an MP. It's important when you are an MP that people listen to what you say and take your appearance for read.'

I met Jane Shilling at her home in Greenwich, and asked her if she was surprised that her article had provoked so much reaction from the female politicians.

Jane Shilling: 'A great many letters were written to the editor, and also a great many to me personally, accusing me of great spite and venom. Most of the letters were saying how dare I write such wicked things about what is a completely peripheral side issue. I thought the contrast between the passion of the letters and the fact that they were still saying this is completely unimportant was very interesting.'

If we accept Jane Shilling's criticisms of the women's clothes as 'unbelievably dowdy', then why did she think they chose to dress like this?

Jane Shilling: 'I think they have been told they must be neat and tidy by whoever it is decides these things. Whips? Mr Alistair Campbell?

'It has been said to them that they have to be jolly neat and tidy and not frighten the horses and the electorate and on no account look revolutionary and shocking and that's why they wear these dire clothes.'

The Members seemed to agree with Shilling's reasoning, even if they liked what they wore and didn't think they looked dull. Member after Member told us that they didn't want their outfits to distract from their message.

Jackie Ballard: 'I think you have to make sure your appearance doesn't distract from your message. Constituents will say, "Oh, I saw you on television," and you'll say, "What was I talking about?" . . . "Oh I don't remember . . . but you looked happy or you looked together or you looked nervous . . ." They give you a sort of feedback on how you looked in general, they don't say you were wearing a red jacket.

'It is important to learn the lesson not to wear incredibly busy clothes, and not to be a complete scruff, so that they are looking at that rather than listening to what you say. So I think if someone looks smart and tidy they tend to have more authority and people listen to what they have to say. If you are in the communications business and you want to get the message across, you have to conform.'

Hazel Blears: 'People have said I've changed dramatically over the last five years. "What have they done to Hazel

Blears?" as if I have been away and had things done to me, which is absolutely untrue. People change and develop and look different as they go through their lives. I think you have a responsibility as an MP to be smart, presentable. You're representing people and they want you to look as if you know what you are doing.'

Hilary Armstrong would not describe herself as a 'clothes freak'. But she admits to being concerned about her appearance, and is determined never to be in 'a position where people are having a go at me because of my clothes . . . But I am not going to have it as an item of contention.'

Dari Taylor: 'I'm a very, very careful dresser. I'm not the smallest woman in the world, consequently I dress very carefully to make sure that my bulk is less visible. I'm reasonably inclined to believe that image is important and people like to see a professional image, therefore I acknowledge that sentiment in my dress, and if I can add a bit of colour to that, it pleases me enormously.

'Three us have bought the same suit in the House of Commons. I said to Glenda Jackson, look, you can wear it on the first and third week, because she's senior to Ann Cryer. Ann can wear it on the fourth week, and I get to wear mine on the second week, so that we are not all looking like triplets in the House. That's the interesting bit about suits, that if you do buy them and it's current fashion, you've got a very high probability of buying the same suit as another woman, whereas on the men, a grey suit looks like a grey suit.'

Perhaps now that there are 120 women members, there should be a register of House of Commons suits as well as business interests. Women determined to make an impact on the Agriculture Select Committee or preparing an important speech from the front bench could consult a book in the House of Commons library before every shopping trip.

Jane Shilling was convinced that men were calling the shots and making the women believe that they had to dress in a certain way to be acceptable: 'A very British attitude, curiously prevalent in all sections of society, holds that it is in poor taste to draw attention to oneself and that by making an effort to look pretty or interesting or to dress well, one is doing just that. "Who does she think she is?"'

Joan Ruddock recalls being called to task for her standards of dress, not by the media, but within Westminster itself. On one occasion a door-keeper advised her 'put a jacket on, madam'. Ruddock complied, 'being somebody who was quite disciplined and obedient, but then afterwards I thought, hell, this is terrible'.

Jane Shilling: 'Men and women, whether in power or not, certainly view clothes differently. Men, as pack animals, like wearing uniforms, whereas women don't. You see it in the City and other industries, where women are now reaching positions of power, and in order to get there, end up wearing what they imagine to be an acceptable version of male uniform. The net result is an extremely uncomfortable and unspontaneous denial of one's femininity.'

Virginia Bottomley agreed that it was just like that when she first arrived at Westminster: 'When I got in, I used to have a grey, a black and a blue suit. I used to wear a shirt which might be striped and I very often wore a bow for a tie. I dressed as near like a man as you can imagine, whereas now the women have come out and they're all in yellow and pink and orange and white, anything to grab the camera's attention. Women have arrived. They're here.'

During the last government, Mrs Bottomley did attract a lot of attention for her willowy English rose appearance. Her Cabinet colleague Gillian Shephard revealed a totally unBritish interest in her image and a passion for designer clothes: 'They decided that Virginia [Bottomley] was the lovely one and I was the other one. They pigeonholed me quite early on as the other one as far as appearance was concerned. So that whatever I wore was [said to be] Marks & Spencer's or Jaeger, or whatever was the best put-down, and in fact my best things were Jean Muir. And indeed I even possess an Armani suit, quite true it's off the peg, but nevertheless it's quite sharp. But you can't have it both ways, I wanted to say, "This is Jean Muir if you want to know!" Maybe the laugh's on me, because on me it looks like Marks & Spencer!'

71

Many of the new women members were a lot less confident than Mrs Shephard and had taken professional advice when they entered public life. A surprising number of women (26 per cent according to the Fawcett Society) confessed that they'd 'had their colours done'. Linda Perham employed an image consultant to help her out some time ago, when she became Mayor of Redbridge.

Jackie Ballard: 'In the last election, the Party did a session at one of the conferences with Mary Spillane (Colour Me Beautiful consultant). I was willing to hate her because she was American and was going to tell me what to look like. But actually I found her very useful. I thought she would say to me, "You are such a mess – you've got to lose ten stone." But she didn't say any of that; she said this is how to make the best of what you are, these are the colours that will suit you. These are the bits you should draw attention to. I don't think you have to look stereotyped, though. If you look at the women in here there is quite a range.

'There are the Barbara Folletts of this world with their green suits and matching shoes and bags who look like they've come out of the cover of *Vogue*. There are lots of others who are pretty tidy but fairly ordinarily dressed. Just wear a jacket rather than a T-shirt, I suppose. I wouldn't wear leggings.'

Candy Atherton also had her colours done before the election, but finds the strains of Westminster life prevent her from spending too much time in front of the mirror. 'To be honest at ten o'clock in the morning, I don't bother. If I'm going into the Chamber, I put the make-up on and if I'm doing TV, I do it.'

Before she became an MP, Barbara Follett helped Labour candidates with their style problems. 'Folletting' was something akin to having one's colours done. 'It's about making sure that the way you look matches what you say,' says Follett, summarising aptly what a number of women expressed. Her style advice employed subtle psychology: 'What I did was simply to say to people – think what your mother would say. Look clean and tidy . . . make sure your hair's cut, washed, brushed. Make sure you've got nothing on that distracts from what you've got to say.' Follett herself, and her style, were a particular target of Jane Shilling. Not that she minds especially. 'I just think it's a pity they can't see beyond the clothes.'

There was such an enormous interest in the new women and their clothes that makeovers were on offer from television programmes and women's magazines.

Liz Blackman: 'I'm not down here to be put in designer clothes and have a makeover and that's how I feel. Everybody has to make their own decision about it. My daughter was absolutely disgusted that I didn't take it. She thought I was being too puritanical, but it wasn't for me. It's not my style.'

Jane Griffiths, Caroline Flint, Shona McIsaac and Diane Abbott looked striking and glamorous in *Elle* magazine.

Jane Griffiths: 'It was lots of fun. I really enjoyed it. Nothing serious about it at all, it wasn't a political statement of any kind . . . just a bit of fun. We were different ages, different shapes and sizes, different colourings, we looked different from each other, and I think it's important to show that all sorts of people can be in politics, our image tends to be of a stuffed shirt-type middle-aged man and it's just not like that any more. It's all changed.'

Valerie Davey: 'The bit I have hated – it's a joke between my election agent and myself – has been photographs. Posing for photographs. The idea that you've got to be much more careful about what you wear, that's the aspect of it, the PR, that I've not particularly welcomed.'

Sandra Osborne went for a makeover on the Richard and Judy show. 'I don't think I would do it again,' was her only comment. She admitted that, during the election campaign, a prospective MP finds herself doing lots of things she wouldn't do normally. 'I ended up doing aerobics at the Hospice Fun Day with Les out of *Coronation Street*.'

Jacqui Smith: 'I don't think we should get bogged down and say "I'm not willing to do anything with the media unless I'm going to be discussing economic policy." There's a whole variety of things we can do and let's be honest about it, more women watch Richard and Judy probably than watch *Question Time*, so if we want to get our message over, we have to use the women's media.'

Shona McIsaac agreed that an added role for women MPs was to act as ambassador for all women. She therefore felt it very important for magazines, newspapers and TV to show them as ordinary women. 'Trying to get the shopping in before going off to work, running round, trying to do the laundry, the vacuuming, living this life as well.'

Most of the women we talked to had extremely busy lives and while they recognised the importance of looking neat and tidy, businesslike and serious, few were willing to confess to getting any real pleasure from clothes. They were often seen as just another task on a long and daunting list. Sally Keeble, the Labour Member for Northampton North, has an admirably rigid clothes-buying plan. 'I go to the sales in July and December and buy three suits at each and that's it.'

Caroline Spelman is a busy mum of three under-fives. She was the only Member brave enough to admit that before the election she went into the Imperial Cancer Research Fund charity shop in her home town of Maidenhead and bought three excellent suits, which she wore throughout the campaign: 'I think it's much more comfortable to live entirely at ease with who you are as a person, so I don't spend vast sums of money on clothes or how I look. I try very hard to look smart and professional, but I devote a very small area of time to that, just because – being a mother with children – there are so many other demands on my time. I think the most important thing is to come across as a professional working mother – because that's what I am.'

At this early stage in their parliamentary careers most of the women seemed to be asking their clothes to do a big job – reassuring constituents, the public and other MPs that they were serious and trustworthy people. It is interesting that the women Jane Shilling praised were all strong personalities and well established at Westminster.

Jane Shilling: 'There are politicians who look absolutely splendid. People I admire tremendously in the House of

Commons – Glenda Jackson, Clare Short, Teresa Gorman. These people look like themselves. Ann Widdecombe is a very interesting case, but I'd say they all look defiant. They don't necessarily look comfortable, what they look is magnificent, like Boadicea. I wouldn't say they looked relaxed.'

Shilling sees clothes as measures of power, the more powerful the person, the more individual the clothes. There can be no doubt that most of the new women at Westminster are nervous and a bit uncomfortable about their clothes and their image. Maybe dressing yourself in pastel-coloured man-made fibres does encourage pastel-coloured man-made thinking.

'The first woman we see floating into the chamber wearing Dolce & Gabanna leopard-skin chiffon will be the first crocus of spring, the first sign that women are really taking over the chamber.' There's no doubt that Jane Shilling's article hurt and upset Westminster women. They were tired and crushed and sensitive and saw it as an early attack from a hostile national press, determined to prove they should never have got there in the first place. Almost to a woman, they were wary of the press and frightened that journalists were 'out to get them'.

5

BABES ON MESSAGE

MORE THAN ANY other group, except perhaps the royal
family, Members of Parliament depend upon a good relationship with the media. Few people attend public meetings these
days, and only a scattering belong to political parties.

To keep his voters in touch with his activities, a politician
has always needed to be on friendly terms with his local
papers, television and radio stations. If he is a Minister or
front-bench spokesman, or even has ambitions in that direction, he needs to develop a relationship with the national
media as well. He'll court the TV producers, flirt with the
journalists, and feed them all juicy morsels from Westminster
whenever he can. Then in his leisure time, the very same
Member, wearing jeans and a sweatshirt, or maybe only his
underpants, will argue that he has a right to a private life. He
demands privacy when his marriage goes wrong, or his
mistress speaks out. He has a difficult balance to achieve,
especially when in good times wives and children appeared
grinning like lottery winners on election brochures and constituency platforms, all in support of the great man.

In August 1997 the Foreign Secretary, Robin Cook was the
most senior politician ever to announce that he was walking
out on his wife.

The Rt Hon. Robin Cook MP (Labour, Livingston):
'Throughout my political life, I have tried to keep my family
out of the public eye. I deeply regret this will cause such public distress to them. I will have no further statement to make
on this matter, and those involved have no wish to make any

comment.

'I accept that I am a public figure, but I would ask that the privacy of those involved be respected at a very painful time.'

The implication is that the toughie politician will take the stick (even though we all know what he does at the weekends is his own business), but his wife and kids must be given space to mourn his departure.

This is not the kind of role model that new female Members, particularly those under thirty, are keen to emulate. Many of them seemed impatient and apprehensive about relations with the press and did not welcome their attentions at all. The new Labour MP for Rochdale, who is only thirty, felt that they had already endowed her with characteristics she neither liked nor recognised.

Lorna Fitzsimons: '[They portray me as] a right-wing shit bag. Careerist, shallow, you name it. I find it highly disturbing that women are judged like that and men aren't. I know men who got as much press coverage as I did, but they are not called careerists or media hussies. But because I'm a woman, because I'm young, it clearly means I'm ambitious.

'It was some of the chauvinistic papers, *Tribune* and *Private Eye*, not too keen on their facts, they spoil a good story. They don't know me. I don't have much respect for them. They're not interested in achieving anything, they're interested in pulling things down. It's fascinating to see you're judged as a shallow right-wing careerist, and yet I've probably got more politics in my little finger than a few of them.

'It's tawdry. Well . . . I'm not going to be the Marie Antoinette of modern-day politics.'

The *News of the World* magazine made a double-page spread out of Lorna's confrontational relationship with the press. 'I May Be an MP, But I Need More Sex' was the headline of Bibi Lynch's article on 19 October.

Lorna had consented to a serious discussion about her first five months as an MP, and during the interview, had made a few jokes about the sorts of thing she could no longer get away with doing or saying. These included an exciting revelation about a late night soap-session with other women in the

Member's Showers. 'These men came in – you should have seen their faces,' and the revelation that she is a deeply sexual being, given to philosophising, 'Cor! I wouldn't mind giving you one,' when she sees an attractive man. She also reminisced sadly over the things she could no longer do: 'I can't have alfresco sex, three in a bed, or get totally out of it on drugs – not that I did. Multiple affairs? Forget it. All those things. All those sexual fantasies and you can't do them because they might become newsworthy.' The next day, the Labour Party issued a statement on Lorna's behalf. She was sad, it said, that the paper had obscured a long and detailed interview about her work as an MP by concentrating on a casual joke she had made to the journalist.

The MP for Bethnal Green and Bow, who's in her twenties, did not enjoy the media attention either.

Oona King: 'Every bit of media coverage you get generates more work and my staff and myself simply cannot cope with the amount we are getting at the moment. I appeal to a greater range of groups round the country – Black, Jewish, young women, all of those. We are just getting too much to be able to deal with them in the manner I would wish to deal with them. So I have realised that the way to deal with this is to become a media hermit. I am doing my best by trying to turn down anything I reasonably can.'

The youngest woman in the House, the new Member for Watford, also disliked the press and wanted as little to do with them as possible. When I arrived in her office a few minutes late for the interview, she had her briefcase under her arm, and was just about to leave. She said she knew nothing about my appointment, which had been arranged with her staff, so she sat down again very reluctantly. She said straight away that she thought the press were too intrusive, always wanting to know more than she wanted to tell.

Claire Ward: 'If somebody asks me am I married, or am I single, or am I seeing somebody – I might say I am single and that's that. But to then go on and ask details about previous boyfriends or who I might be interested in! I do not think it is any business of theirs and certainly not relevant.

'It makes you very conscious of things, and I also find it very irritating that they're not looking in the same way at the men, and I just feel that it's disgraceful chauvinism which allows the media to stereotype women. To look at us as if we are not serious politicians, that we are just here to decorate the benches and be fashion models.'

Will these women continue to feel hostile to the press in the distant day when Labour is less popular, majorities are tight and there's an election to win? Will they start separating their friendly local papers who keep MPs' activities, hard work and achievements in front of their constituents, from the Fleet Street scandal-mongers?

Some women positively enjoyed the light-hearted side of press publicity and knew how to use it to their advantage. Jacqui Smith, Shona McIsaac, Jane Griffiths and Caroline Flint appeared looking drop-dead glamorous in makeovers on television and in women's magazines. They all recognised the value of a bit of popular publicity, but thought the journalists should treat them first and foremost as serious politicians and not just as 'lady Members'.

Caroline Flint declared herself 'ready to throttle the next journalist who asks me about the toilets and crêches in the House of Commons'. The media are, according to her, blind to the important issues. 'There are enough toilets for women MPs . . . and as for the crêche – there are very few women with children under five. They should focus on the diversity of women in Parliament. We are a mixed bunch, and hopefully in many different ways represent the variety of women in Britain. That's what the media should concentrate on.'

But women in large numbers on the green benches at Westminster were new and exciting for the press. Bridget Prentice has been an MP since 1992. In her new capacity as a Government Whip, she had to deal with crowds of media types eager to find out more about her new colleagues: 'In the first couple of days, there were a lot of correspondents who'd be standing in the lobby with me and saying, "Who's that? Go and find out who that one is," as they tried to get to know the new Members. They tell me that watching down from the gallery, it's different. The colour. It's not just people in grey suits They find it quite mesmerising. They see a change already.'

Anne Begg, who has Gaucher's disease, found herself the centre of attention for a while: 'The Blair Babes picture. All of us on the step. These people didn't know who I was. Here was an MP in a wheelchair! And they swooped on me! ITN News, Sky News, they had no idea who I was. I just suddenly appeared out of nowhere. It hadn't occurred to them that someone was standing in a winnable seat in a wheelchair! So I was bombarded for a fortnight with various press things and I thought – when do I get out of this?'

Nearly all the women felt that the press treated the women differently from men, and they all wished it was not so.

Candy Atherton felt that the media tended to target women and subject them to a disproportionate amount of attention. However, she is relatively philosophical about it all: 'I think we always were aware that this would happen. We are a target group and I am told the tabloids are desperately looking for stories about us.' And any old stories, however daft and unlikely. The serious-minded Environment Minister Angela Eagle was joined in the House by her equally serious twin Maria, an expert in housing law. They both wear neat hair, careful suits, shirts and flat shoes for work at Westminster. The media's response? The *Daily Star* carried an article on Maria and Angela, headlined 'New Labour, New Crumpet'.

Maria Fyfe thought she was going to have tough, weighty questions to answer when she got a call from the *Sun*: 'I arranged to meet the reporter in my committee rooms along with my election agent, and this guy turned up with his photographer holding a red rose in his hand, and what he wanted to do was compare and contrast me with another woman, who was the Tory candidate in Renfrew. I assumed he meant politically, but no, she was blonde and I was black-haired and would I allow a photograph to be taken with a rose in my hair? I said no. Then he asked me if I would hold it in my teeth? I said no, but I'll hold it in my hand. Of course, they never used the item.'

Only a few women welcomed the press attention, and they tended to be people who had worked as councillors and dealt mainly with the local and regional press. Louise Ellman was leader of Lancashire County Council until 1 May.

Louise Ellman MP (Labour, Liverpool Riverside): 'I've always worked hard to have good relations with the press, and there are times they print stories and you wish they wouldn't, but overall I think it has been a good experience, because I realised years ago that, unless you can communicate what you are doing or trying to do, people are not aware of what's happening. And the thing that irritated me most was people saying you don't do anything. So I worked hard to make sure people knew what I did, even if they disagreed with it.'

Many of the high-profile women MPs, who had been Members for several years, felt that the national press, and particularly the tabloids, had given them a hard time.

Teresa Gorman: 'I think they've been absolutely bitchy, particularly in the early stages, partly I suppose because I was very outspoken and said things which are not the kind of things that most politicians say. I think most men politicians tend to be very cautious because they don't want to upset their peer group, and so they probably say nothing at all. But just my appearance, just my age, just the fact that I'm very keen on HRT in a health context for women, has given other women the opportunity to be incredibly bitchy about me. And I feel very sad because it's difficult enough to be a woman and get this far without other women trying to drag you down and I think they do us a great disservice. I hope they are only doing it at the behest of male chauvinist editors, but I'm not sure sometimes whether they don't quite enjoy it.'

Clare Short: 'I think the British press is quite backward, and there are some women breaking through in tabloid newspapers, but they are only being allowed through if they behave as badly as the boys at the moment. I think having more women in politics helps, because it's just going to be normal being a woman with the characteristics women have. They won't feel the need to keep commenting on them. I feel it will take more women coming through in journalism really, to really deal with it.'

Virginia Bottomley was a Cabinet Minister in John Major's government and was seldom out of the papers for five years.

Virginia Bottomley: '[There's a] person that nearly all my friends would recognise – someone serious, deeply dedicated, sometimes a bit relentless but who deeply wants to get it right, and very much a team worker. None of those characteristics are really reflected in my press cuttings. There's no point complaining. I feel very privileged to have done the jobs I have done, but I do think women pay quite a high price.'

Diane Abbott sees a better future. 'One hopes, with the critical mass of women, that we have moved beyond that stage.' The critical mass is much talked about at Westminster. Will 120 women be enough to change attitudes? Will female Members stop being a novelty and get the same treatment as the men?

Joan Ruddock thinks not. In her view, the more that women have tried to demonstrate their equality, and the greater the efforts of the Party to ensure equal representation, the more the press attacked them. 'Newspapers investigating women politicians tended to go tangentially at that person as a woman and to use a particularly sexist technique . . . diminish her as a political figure.' The *Daily Mail*'s 'Blair's Babes' was, according to Ruddock, an example of precisely this 'rather snide, undermining approach'. To refer to a group of powerful women as 'babes' – all of whom have had to struggle in order to be elected, and will continue to struggle, 'because the job is a hard job' – is, in her view, nothing short of 'appalling'.

Double standards in the press extend to House of Commons wives as well, as Christine Hamilton discovered after the Battle of Knutsford Heath. 'If you're a man and you stand your ground and you're tough and you're a little bit aggressive people expect it, that's what men are there for. But if a woman does it, she's immediately singled out.

'People have remarked on the way I've stood by Neil, which, to me, was the most natural thing in the world. And my response – when people say, "Why did you do it?" – is what would you have done if your husband was described as a liar, a cheat and corrupt? I know the truth. I know what happened and I know what didn't happen, and I will fight for Neil and for the truth to the bitter end.

'Being called a battle-axe was the nicest thing that was said about me during the election. I was described as "The Wife from Hell" and "The bossy Tyrant" and "The Monstrous Liability". To describe me as Lady Macbeth was an insult to Lady Macbeth according to one commentator.'

A few weeks after the election, I wrote to all 120 women Members and asked them if they would be interviewed for this book. The letter said that someone from my office would phone them in a week or so to make an appointment. The very same day that the letter arrived at Westminster, we were telephoned by Helen Brinton, the new MP for Peterborough, excited at the prospect and saying she'd be delighted to be interviewed. I knew Helen a little. She had been a friend of Bryan Gould and worked with him in the Full Employment Forum. I was delighted she had phoned us, her enthusiasm made the task of interviewing so many women in a short time seem less daunting.

The last time I had seen Helen was several months before at the *Tribune* dinner. She had looked very glamorous and confident, and was wearing lashings of cerise-coloured lipstick which, to my amazement, stayed in place throughout the meal. New Labour, new lipstick. I asked her how she did it. My own lipstick hardly gets past the salted peanuts, let alone the soup. No matter what time it is, when you arrange to meet Helen, she always looks immaculate and her lipstick is very much in place.

We met in the Central Lobby of the House of Commons early on the morning of 2 June. She had been an MP for just four weeks, but she already knew her way around and had booked a committee room off St George's Hall for our interview. She was very nervous and very tired. She told me straight away that her relationship with her husband and kids was going through a difficult patch because she had become an MP.

83

Helen Brinton: 'My husband is five years older than me and had been teaching longer, so whenever there was a promotional move, it was his promotional move, and I followed. There was a sense of resentment on my part and thinking, oh I don't have the opportunity to choose whatever job I want to do. When I went into the Labour Party, it wasn't the idea of being an MP, you know. It was sort of wanting to establish a separateness.'

But she seemed to have acquired much more separateness than she bargained for. Her husband was cross and reckoned that three-quarters of family responsibility now fell on him. The kids were embarrassed and all of them, husband and children, had refused to come to her constituency during the election campaign. She had had to live on a rapidly increasing overdraft and she still had not been paid. Her warmest words were for her understanding bank manager. I felt very sorry for her. Then she told me that she had also begun to have troubles with the press.

It all started when *Newsnight* were looking for a new MP to take part in a discussion on the Queen's Speech. Helen was at home eating a tin of soup and wearing her jeans when the call came. She got back into her MP gear and high-tailed it to the studio.

'Peter Snow was chairing the debate and the last question was about Peter Mandelson and his new role in the government, and Anthony Howard, the political commentator, said didn't we think Peter Mandelson was rather like George Wigg? And then the spotlight went on me. Did I think he was like George Wigg? Now George Wigg was a discredited Minister for lots of reasons in the Wilson government, but most of all he was actually prosecuted, but unproven, as a kerb crawler. Of course I defended Mandelson. I would do it again. He was an arch strategist and his strategy worked for the election. And that was my downfall.'

Matthew Norman, the *Guardian*'s gossip columnist happened to be watching: 'We saw her on *Newsnight* shortly after the election. She was one of the first New Labour MPs allowed out by Millbank and she gave this really extraordinary performance, for which she stayed on-message the entire time, but so aggressively on-message, and reacted so ferociously, however vague the perceived criticism of the leadership, that we got the idea she must have been programmed, and was doing this either by remote control, or according to some microchip.'

Of course Helen had not been sent to *Newsnight* by Labour Party officers at their Millbank HQ. *Newsnight* staff had been ringing round, trying to find a new girl for the debate and Helen was the first they stumbled on who sounded as if she might have something to say. Matthew Norman was wrong. But Helen was wrong too. Over-enthusiastic, eager to begin her glittering TV career, she overreacted to a witty comment by political insider Anthony Howard about a now-forgotten Sixties politician, and made an unnecessary and far too spirited defence of the leadership.

Matthew Norman: 'Then she appeared on an *After Hours* programme – a little round-table chat about work and employment, and we thought that she went off message briefly, there had been some malfunction in the circuitry, which was probably something to do with the studio lights and heat, in which she implied that all unemployed people were sort of work-shy scroungers.'

Matthew Norman began writing about Helen on an almost daily basis in his *Guardian* gossip column. According to him she was an android, a clone from Millbank:

Many who saw Peterborough MP Helen Brinton are convinced she is a cybernaut under the control of Mandy Mandelson. 'It wasn't just the hair or eyes, or how she clucked robotically at any criticism of the leadership,' says one shell-shocked viewer, 'it was the way she recited the five main pledges, and even used the phrase, "Now look!"'

When our meeting on 2 June ended I left feeling full of sympathy for Helen. She was having a tough time with her family, who didn't like her being an MP, she was broke, and the *Guardian* was enjoying poking fun at her undoubtedly naïve performances on television. Other women MPs I spoke to at the time were sympathetic and supportive. Anne Campbell declared the *Guardian* pieces 'vindictive and nasty' and threatened to stop buying it. She felt it was a clear-cut example of discrimination. 'Simon Hoggart has run this rather seedy piece about Michael Fabricant, but it's nothing like as vindictive as the stuff that's been written about Helen. It's an example of male journalism actually discriminating against women, I think.'

I ran into another political journalist at the local swimming pool. She said that Brinton had now made herself a figure of fun in the lobby. 'Would you believe she was handing her card out to journalists?!' I judged from the tone of this remark that MPs were not expected to be card carriers. Once again, because of her enthusiasm, Brinton was an object of derision. Things got worse. Matthew Norman asked any of his readers with previous knowledge of Brinton to write to him. Letters written by Helen to someone in her local constituency party back in 1990 were forwarded to the *Guardian*:

The following extract comes from a missive sent in 1990 by Labour's then prospective parliamentary candidate for Faversham to a senior member of the local Party. Helen had just returned from a meeting with employment spokesman Tony Blair. She asked two questions, 'and then to the buffet and the booze (need to be dignified now and let them come to me). I decided not to rush up to Tony B. – didn't need to – he made a beeline!! We absolutely hit it off. As in house on fire. His words: "It is so great to meet a PPC of such quality. I'm really looking forward to working with you in the House!"'

According to Helen, they were personal letters. 'They are silly, bouncy, bubbly. You know, "I am excited, aren't things going well?" sort of letters.'

Other journalists took up the chase. Simon Hoggart called Helen a 'toughie blonde' and 'brown-nose pursuivant'. In *The Times* Matthew Parris said she was a 'demented parrot'. The

Financial Times began using 'Brintons' as a measure of syco-phancy on a scale of 1 to 10 – with 10 being the MP for Peterborough. Ciaran Byrne and Richard Woods in the *Sunday Times* printed a graphic of a Brintometer with their article. There was a triumphal photo of Brinton with husband and an election-style swingometer claiming to measure fawning, creeping and sycophancy. The article simply gathered together all the growing pile of anti-Brinton press and reprinted it.

I saw Helen again on 10 July. She'd lost a bit of weight, she was heavily made up, the lipsticked mouth seemed huge, her eyes flashed and she seemed very stressed and nervous.

'It's been very hurtful,' she told me. 'Before you're actually in this situation, you might read the Norman column and perhaps have a laugh. You don't know these people. But if you suddenly ARE one of these people, you get to six o'clock in the morning and you do your hair, have your cornflakes and then it's time to get your newspaper. I can't read the *Guardian* any more. I stopped buying it. I open it and I feel sick and I wonder what is going to be in there today. So it's actually taken reading pleasure away from me and you wander round and you look at your colleagues and you think – well, have they read it? What do they think? . . . It's not much fun reading that about yourself in the newspaper, particularly when I feel that newspaper has done nothing to actually find out about me, about my political beliefs, or about me as a person.

'I have fought all my life for politics and I'm not about to stop now. I don't think I have ever been the sort of Labour woman that was appropriate for whatever was in vogue. I am not now, and I can't see that I ever will be, but that's not stopped me. I have got here and I intend to stay. I intend to do what I want to do for the constituency, for the Party, I'm not being put off by that.'

She seemed sad, hurt and defensive, but I sensed that she could also see that she was her own worst enemy. Her kind of passion and enthusiasm, her total lack of cool, simply doesn't fit with New Labour. I cannot really see why Matthew Norman believed she was a Millbank clone: to me she seems exactly the opposite.

At Westminster the Party thought the way she did things was inappropriate; not their sort of girl either. Some experienced Labour Members felt sorry for Helen Brinton and took her aside to give her some good advice. 'Keep quiet,' they said, 'and let it all die down.'

On the last day before the summer recess, I ran into my political journalist friend at the swimming pool again. She said she'd rethought the situation on Helen Brinton. Perhaps she wasn't so bad after all. This puzzled me, until I saw her report that night on the television news, an end-of-term piece on the new Members. There was Helen Brinton being outspoken about her first few weeks. She was interesting, clear and articulate, provocative. In other words, good television.

I asked Matthew Norman if his campaign had anything to do with the fact that Brinton was female. He said it was possible that because she was a woman she had some novelty value, but he felt that if a man had behaved in such a spectacular fashion, he'd have made it into the column too. Was Brinton, then, the most noticeable of the new Members?

Matthew Norman: 'Well, apart from Martin Bell, for very different reasons, yes. She's the one that's caught the eye, and people have gone round having seen her on telly saying, "God, did you see that?" There's a sort of ferocity and automatic quality to her, being on-message, that led to this belief.'

Did he think he had hurt her?

'I think there's every possibility. I wouldn't have thought she likes it. My responsibility is not to worry about whether I'm upsetting a politician. If you go into politics . . . you make a lot of enemies on the way – she's made a spectacular number of enemies, so it seems, then you have to take the knocks and if you then behave in the most sycophantic way, so that your very name is a measure of sycophancy and a measure of how other MPs are judged, then you're going to have to take it.'

Helen Brinton was used by the media, who were fascinated by the new women MPs and eager to find one they could poke fun at. She was rubbished for her naïve enthusiasms, but she had shown that she was media-friendly, ready to drop everything to appear on the television. Journalists know that when the going gets tough, and everyone refuses to comment on an issue or is out of town, the media-friendly MP (they are known in the trade as Rentamouths) will always do you a turn. The problem for Helen Brinton is that she may be back in the press's good books, but her bad start was witnessed and commented on by her fellow MPs. And memories are long at the Palace of Westminster.

The final instalment of the Brinton story (so far) was an article in the *News of the World* of 12 October 1997. 'MP Sues Hubby Over Sex Diary – in one day, he slept with his lover and his mistress . . . then went to bed with his wife', claimed the headline of a double-page spread. Helen is said to be divorcing her husband for adultery: the second female Member to announce plans for divorce since this session began, and the fourth marriage break-up from the government benches since May.

If you are looking at tempestuous relationships between the press and women MPs, the first name that comes to mind is probably Clare Short. The MP for Birmingham, Ladywood has been on the front page and picked over in endless features every year since she arrived at Westminster in 1983. Most politicians are seen as self-interested and often devious, but there is general agreement that Clare is the opposite: straightforward, honest, warm and lovable. She attracts the same kind of unquestioning devotion as the late Princess Diana. People accept she is flawed, makes mistakes, loves too much, but they keep forgiving her and loving her back.

Clare Short's relationship with the press was stormy from the start. Shortly after she arrived at Westminster, she began a campaign against Page 3 girls in the *Sun* newspaper. Young women loved her for it, the tabloids certainly did not, and her fame began to spread. She has had an uneasy relationship with the tabloids ever since, and there was speculation that it might be enough to keep her out of the Cabinet; but she became the Secretary of State for the upgraded International Development Department on 3 May. Ordinary people everywhere were delighted, and so was Clare.

She began to talk immediately of changing the world, of trying to make Tony Blair understand that for very little money Britain could bring big improvements to people's lives in the Third World. Clare began painting her vision of the future on a large canvas. It was barely six weeks before the popular papers dragged attention towards her private life. It seems that all tabloid papers have in their office a file of 'ready to run' damaging stories about politicians on all sides for use on slow news days. The Foreign Secretary Robin Cook for example, was aware that the *News of the World* had a story about him and his secretary a good six months before they decided to publish it.

On 21 July the *News of the World* produced a strange – and to Westminster insiders – tired old story about Clare's dead affair with a Midlands backbench MP. It was just the excuse the *Daily Mail* needed to heap scorn on her all the following week. On the Monday there was a rehash of Sunday's story with the addition of a hugely unflattering (emphasis on hugely) picture, snatched in her constituency the day before.

Clare Short: 'I think there is absolutely no question that women are treated differently all the time. How they look and their sexuality is part of who they are and the press are always making comments, and if they have a go at you, they deliberately choose unflattering photographs. If they are trying to be nice to you, you can see it. They are doing it all the time, making snide comments. With male politicians no one thinks about them as sexual creatures. They're men in suits, they're politicians, until they are caught. I remember the three-in-a-bed bloke and we all looked at him and thought, "Good heavens! Imagine!" because you don't imagine those sorts of things about male politicians. But women's sexuality and looks is always on the front line of the things the press are thinking about. There is a bunch of very sleazy backward men that work around the tabloid press.'

On Wednesday 23 May the *Mail* called her, for no very good reason, 'chillingly selfish' and 'possessively encroaching'. Clare did not respond. On the Thursday Richard Littlejohn turned his column into an agony page full of problems to be solved by 'Aunty Clare':

> Dear Clare,
>   My husband is a politician who has been having an affair
> with a female colleague. I had no idea, even though I was
> working as his secretary at the time. He tells me it's all over
> now, but we are living apart. Can you help?
>
> Sue, Leicester South

Again, Clare did not respond, but she was terribly upset
about the injustice of it all, and had found it very hard not to
fight back. When I went to see her, we stood in the corridor
outside her ministerial office and she seethed. She knew that
anything she said would make it worse, but why had they
taken a tired old story and published it now? Who had been
the leaker? She knew it was not the other MP in the story, he
was just as upset as she was. Who was trying to get at her?
Used to a lifetime of protest and fighting back, Clare felt
unjustly restrained in her new role as Secretary of State.

Just four weeks later came the Montserrat crisis. Between
6,000 and 7,000 Montserratians had left the island since the
first eruptions began in the summer of 1995. The question
facing the Minister for International Development was what
to do with those 5,000 who had chosen to stay behind. In July
delegates from the Montserrat government came to the UK
for talks about the island's future viability. An aid package of
£40 million had already been allocated, but how should the
money be spent? A delicate diplomatic situation was exacer-
bated by the publication, on 16 August, of fresh evidence
which showed that the volcano was even less stable than sci-
entists had previously believed.

Clare, always the people's advocate, felt that the people on
the island were being bullied by some of the local politicians,
who were out for personal gain. So she said so. Exasperated,
she called them greedy and said they would be wanting golden
elephants next. It was a huge mistake. Of course, no one else
seemed to understand that she was making a distinction

between the people of the island and their leaders, and everyone criticised her, even those who said they were her friends. Lesley White wrote in the *Sunday Times*:

> As a long-standing member of the Clare Short defence committee, I am sadly forced to tender my resignation. Throughout the years of inflammatory statements on dope, taxation and sinister spin doctors, she always seemed a politician with a heart of gold and an unfair reputation as a liability. Watching the International Development Secretary's recent whingeing, bullying and pathetic misinterpretation of her Party's macho stance on spending, many of us have changed our minds.

Dominic Lawson in the *Telegraph* used it as a chance to hit out at the government:

> The reward for Miss Short's brilliant interpretation of what Lady Thatcher would have said in the same circumstances, was to be relieved by the Blairites of her command of the Montserrat issue. They could find no fault with the aid policy she had implemented for the volcanically-challenged Montserratians, but it is absolutely characteristic of this government that inappropriate presentation (as they see it) should be the least pardonable of all offences.

Clare, mortified by all this, panicked. And in an exclusive interview with Steven Castle, the Political Editor of the *Independent on Sunday*, on 31 August, she attacked 'vile and dishonest spin doctors' in the government and the Foreign Office as the cause of her bad press. Fortunately for her, all political stories were forgotten that morning, even the one on the front page, as the people of Britain discovered the terrible news from Paris of the death of Diana, Princess of Wales.

Whatever the rights and wrongs of the situation inside the Foreign Office, defending herself in the press, even the friendly part of it, could not help Clare. She restated the government's intention to double the aid budget, to abolish the links between aid and trade, and targeted future aid spending direct to the elimination of world poverty.

Clare Short: 'I'm pleased with the outcome. We spent six months reviewing absolutely everything the Department does and what it should do. The Department feels very proud. We're very sort of united around it. There are now the big challenges to make it happen.

'I think there's a yearning right across the country that was reflected in the election result, and indeed the emotion after Princess Diana's death, for something more decent.'

The Prime Minister is said to agree with her. The Chancellor is backing her spending plans. Clare Short's future in the Cabinet seems secure.

Of the five women in the Cabinet, the Northern Ireland Secretary Mo Mowlam seems to have the happiest and most relaxed relationship with the press. The only way to achieve one, she maintains, 'is be yourself. They'll have you if you're anything else.' And that means being breathtakingly open with everyone. I asked her how she had taken the press articles about her weight gain and her looks before it was revealed that she had been having chemotherapy for a non-malignant brain tumour. She said she had read it, but took no notice.

Mo Mowlam: 'I am a tough old boot. I think we are tough women, my sister's equally tough. I think we just grew up independent and determined to fight. I don't take the highs and the lows, I just float through the middle.'

When the news of her illness broke, she got hundreds of letters from women all over the world: 'Not just [about my] health, it's a funny mixture of letters, it's politics and it's the media and it's views of Ireland and peace . . . it's come from the hearts of all those women. Wonderful.'

Did that make it easier for her to cope with the adverse publicity?

'It made a big difference. But I have always treated the press as human beings and I refuse to complain to them, because if they write bad things, it's part of their job. They are paid by their editors to get bad stories and that's life, and so in that sense you live with it. It's like kicking the messenger – unless they are editors, who I will have a go at. Why get at the boys? It's their job.'

I mentioned Lynda Lee Potter, who has a reputation for treating women MPs harshly and who said of Mo Mowlam before it was revealed that she was ill: 'She's given up smoking and put on two stone. She's developed several chins, shoulders like Frank Bruno, and bears an uncanny resemblance to an only slightly effeminate Geordie trucker.'

Cheerfully, Mo told me she was going to do another interview with Lynda Lee Potter in a few weeks and added: 'I did look a bit like a . . . bus. I was like a beached whale about to take off . . . I looked bad, so in a sense I don't mind. When it's bad journalism, I don't like it . . . The *Sunday Telegraph* has been misreporting us on the peace process – that annoys me because that's irresponsible.'

The Environment Minister Angela Eagle felt that editors sometimes picked female reporters deliberately.

Angela Eagle: 'They always get women to write nastily about women, and I think they do it deliberately so we can't complain that it's sexism from a man. I think those women are probably in an awkward position, in that they are expected to do that sort of thing to keep their jobs and get on, but I do think they ought to examine their consciences.'

Ann Lesley of the *Daily Mail* thinks this is 'utter piffle', of course. 'There isn't an editor born who could make me write something I don't believe. When I write that Harriet Harman is a bossy little milk monitor, that's what I believe.' In that vein, she continues. Blair's babes, male and female alike, are umbilically attached to their pagers, she says, in order to ensure that they remain on-message. The *Daily Mail*, in contrast, is home to a very different breed. 'We say exactly what we want, we say it when we want, and we have no problems with enforcers.'

Angela Eagle, Clare Short and Ann Keen have all been beneficiaries of a strong relationship with one woman journalist, Suzanne Moore of the *Independent*. Moore lives in the same street as Virginia Hayward, Clare Short's adviser and close friend. When Clare Short was reunited with her son Toby Graham, whom she hadn't seen since she gave him up for adoption twenty-five years before, she knew that the story would have to come out, and Virginia Hayward arranged a meeting between her and Moore. There was overwhelming public sympathy for both Clare and her son when Moore's sensitively written piece was splashed across the front page of the *Independent*. All involved were delighted with the result. There was no hostile press for Clare and Moore had a sizeable scoop on her hands. This method of news control worked so well for Clare Short that Suzanne Moore was called in a few months later to break the news that Ann Keen had been reunited with the son she gave up for adoption twenty-eight years earlier. Keen was very nervous about the situation, but her story was also received with sympathy.

In August Angela Eagle had her own good news story to tell, and she too chose to give it to Suzanne Moore. The story this time could not be guaranteed a joyful reception. Angela Eagle wanted to go public about her happy long-term relationship with a woman. Because they were both involved in Labour politics, Angela and her partner had been discreet about their partnership, but now that Angela was a Minister they wanted to set up home together to make the most of Angela's minimal free time. Some papers reprinted Suzanne Moore's article and all the tabloids ran the story, but in the aftermath of Princess Diana's funeral, there was scarcely any follow-up, and no snide comments at all. The *Guardian*, always bang up-to-date with social nuances, published a list of 'in' people and 'out' people, and Angela was definitely in. When *The Times* ran a profile of Chris Smith's partner Dorian a week or so later, in which he gossiped in a suitably house-wifely way about the family pet and his friendship with other Members' spouses, there were some suggestions that the government had a policy of bringing out stories about the gay partnerships of Ministers in the hope of making them acceptable and unremarkable.

Before the 1997 election women who aspired to be MPs needed to present a conventional public image. Those who did not suffered constant hostile attention from the press. In 1974 Maureen Colquhoun was elected the Labour MP for Northampton. Maureen's lifestyle seemed normal enough. She was married to a *Sunday Times* journalist, Keith Colquhoun, and they had two teenage children. She was an outspoken, left-wing feminist and about halfway through her first term she fell in love with the editor of *Sappho*, a lesbian magazine:

> Babs and myself worked very closely together and totally fell in love with one another. By the time the House met to debate the second reading of the Balance of the Sexes Bill on Friday May 16th, 1975, I knew that Babs loved me and I loved her. As I looked up in the gallery that Friday afternoon of the debate I was met by another peculiar situation. Babs Todd and her young daughter Mairi looking down, and Keith Colquhoun a few seats away, totally unaware of the other's presence. (From Maureen Colquhoun, *A Woman in the House*, 1980)

Like Angela Eagle twenty years later, Maureen was an honest woman and wanted the world to know about and accept her changed lifestyle. It helped to ruin her political career. Maureen today presents a conservative image. In a print dress and low-heeled shoes, looking the very image of a modern middle-class grandma, she was waiting for me at the University Women's Club. She talked about her active membership of her local Labour Party in the Lake District and her enthusiastic campaigning on behalf of the National Parks. She was kind about her ex-husband ('lovely man') whom she sees fairly often, and her kids and grandchildren. She was cheeky about her partner Babs, in the way long-term lovers often are. 'As I got on the train, I said to her, "Farewell, my lesbian lover," and she said, "Maureen, don't be so shocking!"'

In her autobiography, Maureen Colquhoun wrote: 'I believe the sweeping stereotyping of homosexuals will only disappear if those who are homosexual come out and say so. There is nothing to hide. Those who remain hidden degrade both themselves and their relationships.' (p.159)

When I told her that a female MP I knew of was thinking of coming out, her reaction was surprising. 'Tell her not to do it,' she said, adamantly. 'She'll never survive.'

I had imagined, having read her book, that she would look back ruefully and see herself as a woman who had arrived on the political scene just slightly before her time. Not a bit of it. Maureen Colquhoun believes that today a woman cannot announce that she is a lesbian and hope to survive in parliament. But what about Chris Smith or Ben Bradshaw? Maureen believes that where male homosexuals have been accepted by society, gay women have not.

When Angela's story was published, I rang Maureen and asked what she thought. She was cautious. 'I don't want to be downbeat for Angela's sake. It's all gone very well for now, but I forecast it won't last. They cannot resist it. What that could do to her relationship could be pretty bad. The other person is a kind of victim. As the MP, you are carrying all before you, fighting the good fight, making the announcements and doing everything. Your partner has their job but they are harassed at work, say, as an example, as a consequence of this coming out. It's very difficult to be a partner.'

Most MPs felt that they would be prepared to take criticism if it related to their work or their policies, but not their private life, and they liked it even less when it came from women journalists. Angela Eagle herself thought it was time to take a stand: 'I don't mind being criticised for my policies or my performances as a minister, but I do mind having my clothes scrutinised constantly or having derogatory remarks made about my hair or something equally irrelevant. They don't do it to men on the whole and I am always disappointed when I see women journalists doing that. I understand that they're in a difficult position – getting on in their own careers – but they should stop and think. There are now enough of us around in public life to start saying no to that kind of thing.'

I went to visit Angela Eagle in her constituency a few weeks after she had told her story to Suzanne Moore. Was she pleased with the way things had gone? 'It was much better than I thought it might be,' she concluded. 'I've had nothing but support from the Party nationally and locally and from constituents.' She speaks especially fondly of her constituency – television crews came up to do vox pops in the constituency and went away empty-handed: 'They couldn't find anyone to say nasty things about me.' She had been intending to announce her relationship after the election, but becoming a Minister meant she had too many other things to deal with. 'I had to work my way through that and ensure that I informed the right people, so I didn't take anyone by surprise.'

She feels that the reactions of Westminster and the public are symptomatic of the times. 'We've had this repressive Conservative government which has been so backward-looking for eighteen years . . . society has moved on. It's almost like time has gone much much faster in the past six months, and society has almost matured and changed very rapidly, because we have had a recognition at the top that changes have taken place. It's an odd feeling, but I feel almost like the last six months is years and years of social progress.'

I told her I had talked to Maureen Colquhoun, who warned that things were often more difficult for partners. Angela said she thought that it was the same thing for all partners and families of MPs. 'I think people often forget that it's the MP who chooses to live a public life. It's not the entire family and I just wish that the media and the people out there would remember that and spare a thought for the families and partners of people who go into public life, because it's a tremendous strain, and they haven't necessarily chosen to deal with it.'

6

HOUSE WIVES

FAMILIES HAVE NEVER been central to life at Westminster: there is only one room and one telephone line for their use in the whole vast complex. The Families Room, just off the Central Lobby, is 600 square feet carpeted in green and panelled in oak, with rose-pink chairs and sofas planted in neat rows. Roughly one square foot of space for every Member's family. An oak-framed notice says: 'This room is for the use of Members' wives and Lady Members' husbands, and if space permits, other close relatives of Members.'

There are about 600 spouses and partners and 2,000 children of Members, so one might expect the room to be crowded, but families hardly flock to Westminster. Apart from the 'Secretary Spouse' species – for example, Biddy Cash, wife of Bill (Conservative, Stone), Maggie Ashton, Joe's missus, and Christine Hamilton, controller of Neil (the former Conservative MP for Tatton) – most stay away, waiting for the political crisis when their husband suddenly announces he wants to spend more time with them (Norman Fowler); the sexual scandal when a reassuring family photograph is required (David Mellor); or the *bombe surprise* (Robin Cook).

Often the only occupant of the Families Room is a left-over Old Labour wife hunched in the corner watching Channel 4 Racing. There can be a mini rush-hour in the early evening when a few Tory wives perch, waiting for busy voting husbands to collect them for dinner.

The only 'facility' is a changing room off the main room. It

99

is stuffy and windowless. There are wash-basins, hand towels and a couple of wooden-backed bristle brushes. The light over the basin does not work. A forgotten frock (Barry Sherrard white coin-spotted polyester size 10) hangs in the corner.

School holidays can bring small groups of children who cluster sullenly round the television waiting for Dad or Mum. A few years ago Joan Walley campaigned to have some children's books provided. *Statesmen Who Changed the World* and *Are You My Mother?* now lie unread alongside *Magica Buenos Aires*.

MPs' spouses and their children under eighteen are entitled to fifteen free rail or plane journeys a year between Westminster and home or the constituency. But once they get to London no one really wants them hanging around the House of Commons. On the last day of the first session of the new parliament, Ruth Kelly was working on the terrace with her assistant, Ross McCauley. Her two-month-old son Eammon was on her lap. At the next table Sally Keeble was being interviewed by an Italian journalist, her eighteen-month-old toddler at her feet. Lord Mason of Barnsley (formerly Labour Northern Ireland Secretary, Roy) swept by with a colleague. 'They're breeding on the Terrace!' he exclaimed loudly.

Westminster specialises in protecting Members of Parliament from the outside world. Ordinary mortals who want to talk to their own representative present a green card at the desk in the Central Lobby. The Member, if she or he is actually in the House, can choose whether or not to respond.

Families at home or in the constituency may, along with everyone else, leave telephone messages which are recorded on to carbonated forms. One copy is carried round the Palace by a uniformed messenger, who searches the lobbies, the library, the bars, the Terrace, for your Member. This can take hours. And the ball is always in the Member's court. If they do not want to respond, or if they are not there at all, then the caller receives no return message.

On the walls of the Families Room are seven large prints of idealised scenes of nineteenth-century family life by William Powell Frith R.A. They were bought to commemorate Roberta

Wakeham, who was killed in the IRA bombing of the Brighton conference hotel when her husband was Conservative Home Secretary. They were presented by the Parliamentary Wives.

The Parliamentary Wives were a Christian Fellowship of women married to Members and Peers, mostly Tory, and were nearly wiped out in the 1997 election. When Janet Boateng's husband Paul became MP for Brent South in 1987, Janet was keen to take part in Westminster life, so she joined the Parliamentary Wives.

Janet Boateng: 'Most of the members were wives of Tory Peers and Tory MPs. I became quite friendly with them because we had a similar interest in being wives with Christian backgrounds. We met every Tuesday in Speaker's House. I did make lots of friends, but I didn't really feel that if I had a problem they were the sort of people I would really want to pour my heart out to. It would have been useful to have known other Labour wives. So, if I was concerned about a specific aspect in relation to the Commons, I could ring up and talk to them about it.'

Buoyed up by Labour's landslide victory, Janet and Bettina Strang, wife of Transport Minister Gavin Strang, got together to set up the Parliamentary Partners Support Group, President Cherie Booth, Vice-President Pauline Prescott. The group will organise family outings, support widows and widowers, mentor new Members and their partners and set up a counselling service for those with problems.

Janet Boateng told me, 'Someone rang up – I think it was Robin Corbett's (Labour, Birmingham Erdington) wife – and said, "Why can't we have a moan line because I find that Members' wives or partners are always moaning about something. We could leave it for the older ones to answer – the ones who've been here for ages."'

Within a few days of the formation of the Parliamentary Partners Support Group, the suicide of Scots MP Gordon McMaster and the surprise announcement by the Foreign Secretary that he was leaving his wife for his secretary suggested that the services of the group could be heavily in demand.

I attended a fringe meeting at the Labour Party conference at which the Foreign Secretary Robin Cook talked about overseas aid and Third World development. Before his arrival muscled heavies in lounge suits cased the joint. Cook swept into the room every inch the senior government Minister. At the back stood a lonely figure in a navy blue suit, carefully assessing his every move: Gaynor Regan, his Commons secretary and recently acknowledged long-term partner. Gaynor, her long brown hair spread carefully on her shoulders, clutched her small black handbag firmly and rocked gently on her medium-heeled court shoes. She looked unhappy.

Equally unhappy in Edinburgh is Cook's wife of twenty-eight years, Margaret, ditched by the Foreign Secretary without warning in early August. Westminster has been pretty tough on both women.

Westminster is tough on the men also, particularly on your average Member representing a constituency out of London. On Sunday night or Monday morning he takes a bag stuffed with fresh laundry and constituency problems and sets out for the capital. The family settles down to their usual busy week, used to Dad being absent from four breakfasts and three or four evening meals. They have their friends around them; the MP, on the other hand, is likely to be lonely.

When Austin was first elected in 1979, the allowance for accommodation in London was tiny, and you were not allowed to benefit from it by using the money to pay a mortgage on a London property, so Members rented cheap rooms, often in groups. I remember Joe Ashton before he moved to the Barbican sharing a bedsit with two other members – Kevin McNamara (Labour, Hull North) and Dennis Canavan (Labour, Falkirk West). Joe used to say it was tough going because Dennis's feet smelled terrible. But they did have company, and they could look forward to going home to their sweet-smelling wives at the weekend.

And then the allowance was improved and Members were allowed to use it to pay off a mortgage. MPs began buying studio flats and sections of converted terraced houses in Vauxhall and Waterloo, lofts in Bermondsey and bedsits on

Millbank. And going home alone in the evenings.

Whatever way you look at it, unless an MP and spouse have a joint parliamentary role as MP and secretary, it is inevitable that two or three nights a week at least, many couples are going to be apart. Christine Hamilton still dreads the prospect of having to spend a night apart from Neil: 'For us, we need to be together all the time. It suits us. Whereas some people would find it awful to work with their spouse, it suited us. It was obviously tremendously exciting. Neil had always wanted to be an MP, ever since he was thirteen, I think, if not earlier, and he'd achieved the first step of his ambition. So it was wonderful, and I loved it, because having been there for so long, it was great to have him there with me.'

Margaret Cook said, in her first letter to the *Scotsman*, that her own punishing schedule in the NHS meant that she did not spend enough time with her husband in London. Many other spouses have probably said something like that to themselves.

So on Sunday nights, or Monday mornings, a lot of spouses send their beloveds off to London for the week. And in the daytime the beloved works away in his office dealing with constituency problems attending the Select Committee on this and that, asking questions, making odd speeches in the Chamber, going to Party meetings. Having lunch with journalists. And his days are full. The evenings start off OK. Drinks between six and seven with the Society for the Protection of Hatblocks and Haberdashers, and then . . .

Some fill the lonely evenings with drink. But a far more common course of action is for the beloved in question to continue his burgeoning relationship with Ms Amanda X, ambitious 23-year-old university graduate, his secretary-cum-researcher-cum-right-hand woman. They'll have a drink together on the Terrace. Such couples are visible every evening: somebody's husband and his attractive assistant, their heads together, working away at a table for two. And presumably they get the same thrill out of the shared work, the same excitement, as any professional man-woman team. But this couple are different because they only have each other. Being an MP is a lonely business, and Amanda X may be the only attainable woman your average overworked, underorganised middle-aged Member for Thatchford East gets close to all week. Of course he knows the journalists in the lobby, the women who work on his regional papers, radio stations and television channels, but they're not together day after day like him and Amanda. Amanda who, only two years out of university, is probably sharing some overcrowded flat in Clapham or Kilburn with other women just like her. So it is quite easy to invite Amanda back to 'the flat' in Vauxhall for supper. She might even offer to cook some spaghetti while the two of them get quite excited about Scottish devolution.

That, in the last twenty years, is the way I imagine it has largely gone. Forget exotic behaviour by stars like David Mellor: until 1 May 1997, most MPs were amiable middle-aged men in suits, representing constituencies outside London with wives and children living elsewhere.

House surgeon Dr Margaret Whitmore married PhD student Robin Cook in Bristol in 1969. She was twenty-five, he was twenty three. They'd met when they were students at Edinburgh university. Their families and wedding guests waved them off on their honeymoon at Bristol Temple Meads station. As the train pulled out Robin unpacked his papers from his briefcase. He warned Margaret to keep quiet for the two-hour journey to London because he had work to do.

Margaret Cook says she realised then that marriage to Robin was going to include coping with his super-sized ego, but she'd fallen in love with his considerable brain power, and maybe the two went together. For twenty-eight years she managed well. They were respectful and controlled in their relationship with each other. They didn't scream and shout, she didn't tell other people when they had problems. The Cooks were a thoroughly modern couple of intelligent high achievers who got on with their own careers during the week and took great pleasure in each other's intellectual strengths as well as their happy family life, when they met at the weekend.

The first thing that strikes you about Margaret Cook is how

pretty she is. She looks at least a decade younger than her age. Her skin is smooth and wrinkle-free. She's warm and responsive. The one newspaper photo I had seen made her look rather academic and earnest, but this is not at all true. Margaret is used to dealing with men. She has two sons and her closest colleagues at the hospital are mainly male. She says they are a tight-knit lot, black humour a speciality, and although she agreed with me that a man and woman working together could have an exciting and close relationship, she said she had never even thought of committing adultery all through their long marriage. She was married to Robin, she knew about his ego, she knew he had had a few affairs in the past, she knew all about Gaynor, but still she was not tempted. She was in love with her husband. When Labour had proclaimed that things could only get better in the lead up to the election, they were right as far as the Foreign Secretary's marriage was concerned.

On 1 August 1997 Robin and Margaret flew from Edinburgh to Heathrow Terminal 1, en route for a riding holiday in Montana. They had both just been involved in domestic tasks, paying bills, cancelling papers, sorting out their diaries, and looking forward to three weeks off. Margaret was particularly happy. When Robin had become Foreign Secretary three months earlier, their relationship had been rocky because of a relationship with his secretary, but all the excitement and the new responsibilities seemed to have finished that. Margaret did not think she needed to ask Robin if the affair was over. He now had at least three security people with him all the time, and he was working fifteen hours a day so, at the very least, when would he have the time?

Married life had been difficult in the months leading up to the election. The Cooks had been together at the weekends as usual, but like a brother and sister. Since Labour's victory all this had changed. Margaret really believed the marriage had been saved. The weekend after the election, Robin and Margaret went to the Badminton Horse Trials together. They had a wonderful time during the day and an intimate dinner alone in the evening. They had always had plenty to say to each other and that evening was no exception. Margaret even allowed herself the luxury of thinking that they were doing pretty well for a couple in their twenty-eighth year of marriage. She remembered other couples she knew, and people she had watched in restaurants, who seemed to have nothing to say to one another after many years together. She and Robin, on the other hand, were getting on really well again, and were back to their old sparring intellectual relationship.

The Cooks then had a happy weekend at Dorneywood, the Foreign Secretary's official residence, and made promises to each other about a better future. They vowed to write time with each other into their diaries until well into 1998. Margaret tentatively asked Robin if she could go with him on the Hong Kong independence trip and he agreed. In a burst of *bonhomie* he invited her to go with him on an official visit to India later in the year. Margaret went cheerfully back to work and booked her leave.

Margaret Cook is a consultant haematologist at St John's Hospital, Livingston, which is in her husband's constituency. She is on call a lot of the time and this makes it difficult for her to take time away from home unless she has planned it a long time in advance. She has never been to a Labour Party conference and she has almost never visited her husband in London. She did not even have a key to his London flat, but she had asked a few times. He never got round to giving her one. In the last couple of years Robin has occasionally been invited to what Margaret calls 'glittering occasions' in London. Sometimes she would say to him, 'Wasn't I invited to that?' and Robin would reply reasonably, 'Well, yes, you were, but as it was mid-week I didn't think you would want to go.'

The pattern of their lives was quite settled. He was away in London or wherever, for most of the week. She was busy at her work in Livingston. She took all the day-to-day responsibility for bringing up their children, for running the house and making sure they had enough money to keep going. Until he became Foreign Secretary, Margaret always earned more than

Robin, and Robin was 'pretty chaotic' with money.

The Cooks' plane from Edinburgh arrived at Heathrow and a Foreign Office car met them and drove them to Terminal 4. On the way Robin's mobile phone rang. It was Alistair Campbell with some instructions. Robin asked if he could use a VIP room at the terminal to talk privately to Margaret. Their luggage had been booked through from Edinbugh to Boston, so it went straight to the plane. Margaret had packed Robin's case for him and as a surprise she'd included a new and expensive pair of leather riding chaps. She knew he would be pleased with them.

Robin shut the door of the VIP room and told Margaret that the *News of the World* had 'got the story'. She understood what this meant, because for a year they had both lived with the knowledge that the *News of the World* had seen Robin and a woman (presumably Gaynor) together in a hotel and they might use the story at any time. They had expected it to surface in the lead up to the election. In the VIP lounge Robin brusquely told Margaret that he had been told he could not leave the country, so the holiday was cancelled and, by the way, so was the marriage.

The Cooks' older son, who lives in the south of England, had turned up at the airport to wave them goodbye. He was ushered into the VIP room. He could see immediately that something was wrong, and asked his mum what the matter was. Margaret told Robin that it was his responsibility to tell Chris. She had never spoken to her sons or anyone else about her marriage problems. Robin then told his son that he was having an affair with his secretary and was leaving Margaret for good.

Margaret says that by this stage in their marriage she had learned that Robin often said things he did not mean, and somehow she hoped this might have happened here. So she went back into town with him and they sat down over a bottle of scotch in the Foreign Secretary's residence at 1 Carlton Gardens and discussed the situation. She realised that he was telling the truth and it really was the end of their marriage. In the dignified way that had characterised their whole marriage, she went quietly off to bed and left without seeing Robin the next morning.

She and her son Chris flew back to Edinburgh. It was a Saturday morning and they only had a few hours to prepare themselves before Robin announced their marriage was over, and the story about Robin and Gaynor was published in the *News of the World*.

Margaret Cook knows very little about Gaynor. She has never asked, she does not really want to know. She says she often refers to her as 'that woman' and blames her for stealing her husband. But, most of all, she blames her husband for his super-shiny ego. She feels that what he wants and needs is the support of younger women who adore him and look up to him. What he cannot cope with is the give and take of a modern marriage between two intellectual equals, equal in the workplace, equal in the support mechanisms they put in place for each other. Perhaps he agrees with her. He has told her that he is frightened of her. Frightened of her strength and her independence.

I am in the same age group, I am married to a Labour MP. The story seems much like my own. One man, one woman, one ego (his). But there the resemblance ends. Our marriage is nothing like the Cooks'. We have fought and scrapped and bickered our way from the 1960s to the 1990s, with me compromising with the male ego on the 'you lose some, you lose some more' basis. Austin always asks when I give in gracelessly, 'Why on earth didn't you do so at the beginning and avoid the row?'

The Cooks always behaved with dignity and respect for each other. They never had rows and Margaret never gave in irrationally.

Robin is the *Glasgow Herald*'s racing tipster, a post which Margaret says started out as a bit of fun, but Robin soon became deadly serious and obsessive about it. He had to phone his tip and his column into the paper at five o'clock on a Friday afternoon.

One Friday afternoon, Margaret had an emergency about a blood transfusion at Livingston hospital. She ordered some tests and set off for home in the twenty minutes it would take for the work to be done. As soon as she got home, she picked up the phone and Robin asked her to put it down because he needed to phone in his column. Margaret explained she had an emergency, a life was at stake. Robin still wanted to phone his paper first. Margaret insisted and picked up the receiver.

I admired her greatly for this. I would have started out in the right way, stating my case, hoping reason would be enough. Met by a male ego and a refusal to compromise, I'd have lost my temper, ranted and railed, then given in, dashed out to find a phone box and installed a second telephone line the next week.

Margaret won a housing battle on rational grounds too. Robin has always wanted to live in the elegant and beautiful Newtown area of Edinburgh. (Interestingly Robin and Gaynor have been seen flat-hunting there.) Margaret defeated him on this one too, pointing out that where they currently lived was nearer to the constituency, and she had a far shorter drive to work.

When she arrived back in Edinburgh on 2 August 1997, Margaret had three empty weeks and a whole new life without Robin in front of her. There was lots of sympathetic mail, including a hand-written letter from Tony Blair saying that both he and Cherie were very sad and supportive about the pressures of press and public attention that Margaret had had to put up with. Margaret Cook picked up her pen and fired right back. How kind of them. Perhaps they were also sad and supportive about her ruined marriage?

The Blairs were on holiday in Italy at the time, but within hours of the letter arriving at Number 10, PM without Portfolio Peter Mandelson was on the phone to Margaret. He had talked to Tony and Tony was really sorry that there had been a misunderstanding and he was planning to write again. Margaret said she didn't want another reply, that she had actually written because she was sure Tony would have lots of letters to write to erring Cabinet Ministers' wives during his premiership and she just wanted to make sure he got it right next time. And while he was on the line and appreciating the important part that he and the Prime Minister had played in the end of her marriage, what she would really appreciate would be a visit from the Minister without Portfolio himself. Mandelson, presumably On Message as a Relate Counsellor, duly turned up on Margaret's front doorstep a few days later. He was, she says, absolutely charming. Did he say anything? Well, nothing that meant anything, but he was lovely.

Margaret Cook accepts that her marriage is over for good. She says cheerfully that she would certainly never marry again. A team of toyboys? Yes please. But all the effort that goes into building a twenty-eight year marriage, certainly not.

Westminster worked against her. Every week her husband was in London alone while she was in the constituency, working in a demanding job in the Health Service, bringing up her sons. When he arrived home at the weekend, she wanted him to see that they both needed the support the other partner could offer. Her husband, she felt, always really wanted something else. He wanted love and support – adoration really, but he was far too busy to return it.

Women MPs who had been working at Westminster before the 1997 election were only too aware of the problems of combining a family with political life.

Virginia Bottomley: 'If a woman wants to go into political life, she needs to feel comfortable with herself, and I think, for a woman more than a man, that means feeling comfortable with her partner, with her friends and her family. I have been fortunate to have had no ambivalent messages from my nearest and dearest. Both my daughters have very strong personalities, I think one of them may go into politics and there isn't any ambivalence – I don't think there is for younger women now. But I'm very aware that at the time I was going in, for many women, their husbands were fairly hostile, as were their families and friends.'

Young children are top of the potential problem list, starting the day they are born.

Diane Abbott: 'I came in when he was eight days old, for a vote. It's called a three-line whip. I took him through the lobby in one of those little slings and they said, "You can't. Strangers aren't allowed in the lobby." This shows you how much the English hate children – David Blunkett's dog was allowed in the lobby, but my baby wasn't.'

Barbara Castle remembers fighting for a better deal for Helene Hayman when she was a nursing mother at Westminster. This was in the 1970s, when Labour had a very small majority and voting went on long and late. Barbara Castle saw Hayman, in a very advanced stage of pregnancy, 'waddling through the Division Lobby at two in the morning. I said, "My sweet child, you ought not to be here." She said, "Margaret Thatcher's being very tough and the Tories won't give me a pair." So I stormed off to see Margaret Thatcher and we eventually got Helene a pair.' When the child was delivered, the women sacrificed one of their small reading rooms at the back of the Speaker's Chair so Hayman would have somewhere private to feed her baby.

Now Labour Roads Minister, Baroness Hayman disagrees with the above account:

'The story's actually funnier than that. I was very pregnant – it was the long hot summer of 1976. There was no pairing at all because Michael Heseltine had waved the mace around at Whitsun . . . and we were running three-line whips on Lords' amendments to very contentious legislation, all the aircraft and shipbuilding and education. At two o'clock in the morning, I was quietly lying in the Lady Members' Room, trying to have some peace with the light out and Barbara came in and found me there. She decided that this was not what the Pankhursts had been all about and she marched into Humphrey Atkins's office and told him that if anything happened to me or my child, it was his personal responsibility – and marched out again.

'Then I had Barbara come back, to say that she had done this and it was all going to be sorted. Then I had Michael Cox, who was the Chief Whip, march in, not well pleased, saying that Humphrey Atkins was saying to him he'd got the Prime Minister there and the Foreign Secretary, so why should he send me home? Then he went out again, very unhappy, and so I was terribly unhappy because he was unhappy and shouting and cursing me. And then Margaret Thatcher walked in. I'd never spoken to her before in my life. She said, "I have a sore throat. You are pregnant. We're both going home."

'So she marched out again, and I'm still there not knowing if I can go home because Margaret Thatcher says I can go home, and finally Michael Cox came back – and by this time he was absolutely incandescent with rage and said, "Not only have I got to send you home, I've got to send you home in my bloody car!"

'After the baby was born on 25 October, I had intended to have till after Christmas off. But because there was no pairing, and we had no majority, they said – you're going to have to come in – this was when the baby was a week old. Then I personally wrote to Margaret Thatcher and asked her to let me pair. But they were adamant. I was upset because of all the stuff that came out then . . . horrid publicity: I was "brandishing" this baby and I'd "decided to go and breast-feed to make a political statement" and everything. It was nothing to do with that at all. It was down to the fact that I wasn't allowed any time off, and I wasn't going to be responsible for the government losing its legislation. That's why Joe Ashton had that scene in his play.'

In Joe Ashton's play, *A Majority of One*, Margaret Thatcher objects to Hayman breast-feeding.

'I never actually saw it. There was a wonderful cartoon of Jim Callaghan crossing New Palace Yard with a carrycot and Majority of One on the side . . . Very sweet because all the other cartoons were really horrid – you know, mainly centred around breasts.

'It wasn't just me – people were coming in on their life-support machines in ambulances, and I was just caught up in that. A lot less badly off than other people.

'The other thing is – you will have Tory MPs who say they saw me breast-feed in the Chamber. Now this is a nonsense . . . the baby never went into the Chamber. When I lost my seat, one of the door-keepers told me that he had been advised by the Serjeant-at-Arms as to the degree of force he was allowed to use to stop me taking the baby into the Chamber if I tried to.

'All I did was come in with the baby, because we were on running whips and I was feeding him and he was ten days old and I wasn't going to leave him. I sat in misery in the Lady Members' Room and was either nodded through, or I left the baby there sometimes with a policeman while I nipped to vote, but it was no major political statement . . . some great blow for breast-feeding in public.'

But even if she had no time to make radical statements, Hayman agrees that Westminster was a tough environment for women: 'There were very few young women MPs at that time – we always got taken for secretaries . . . absolutely par for the course. You did get patronised – that was very much how young women were treated . . . in the professional world. Who knows whether it's changed or not.

'I do think the sheer numbers this time must make a difference.'

The woman MP has all the problems of a working mother and then some. Some of the women who won London seats said that the location factor was all-important to them, and that they wouldn't have stood if the only seat available was far from London. Others moved their families to their constituency, so that most of the travelling would be done by the Member, and the children would have a stable base and not much travelling. The worst option of all is for the family to live in a third place. Then a kind of 'parliamentary triangle' is formed with the MP constantly travelling between all three points.

Joan Walley: 'Like any woman who works full-time, you're juggling the time you've got between work and home. In the case of an MP, there's usually a third dimension and that's the needs of the constituency. It's almost like being Superman, changing into different suits to become a different person. It's the transition from living in an area, at home, taking the kids to school, being a mum, and then having to come down here to Westminster.'

113

When Joan Walley was selected for Stoke-on-Trent North, she and her husband and sons moved from London and set up their family home in the constituency. 'It was absolutely the right decision to make. We wanted to have a secure family home and we wanted to be part and parcel of the constituency. We wanted to make that link, so that we were firmly here in the constituency where it really mattered. Any working woman has to make sacrifices and we all do it. I admit I miss my family enormously when I'm away in London and I wish there was another way to do it. I hope that the women coming in now don't have to go through what I've gone through. My husband took on a much bigger role as a house-husband. He's there for the children. He's now full-time at home, dealing with everything while I'm away and it's just an example of how we've worked our partnership out together.'

Gwyneth Dunwoody and her late husband John became MPs in the same election. They moved their children to London. 'I ran everywhere,' she admits. 'Looking back on it, I don't quite know how I did it.' An arrangement with the Whips enabled her to go home at about six in the evening, to make sure everything was OK. The children attended state schools in London: one went to the comprehensive in Putney and two to a primary school in Victoria.

Gwyneth Dunwoody: 'I had a hilarious exchange with Margaret Thatcher on that subject. I was talking to my children on the phone, that sort of motherly thing: "Turn the television off! Stop fighting! I'll be there in a minute! Do your homework!" She overheard and obviously couldn't understand – she said to me: "Where are your children?" and I said, "Well they're at home." She said, "No, no where do they go to school?" And I suddenly realised we were not in the same life . . . she couldn't imagine that you could have children at a state school and be a Member of Parliament. Mind you, it took a bit of doing.'

When my husband Austin became the MP for Grimsby in 1977 things grew very difficult. We were living in Sowerby Bridge in West Yorkshire, conveniently equidistant from

Granada Television in Manchester, where I worked, and Yorkshire Television in Leeds, where Austin was a presenter on the local magazine programme *Calendar*. Part of our house had been turned into a separate flat and Austin's parents had just moved in with us. Then there were our twins, Jonathan and Hannah, aged nine, and their nanny Lynda, who had been with us for eight of those nine years. She had just become a live-out nanny, having married a local man and set up home not far away. Then in Oxford there were Susan and Nicola, Austin's daughters from his first marriage, and their mum, Pat. Trying hard to be a father to them too, Austin was spending every second weekend in Oxford. Into this equation add the fact that the new MP for Grimsby had announced at the beginning of his campaign, and repeated frequently throughout it, that if he was elected, the family (this was assumed to mean the speed-dial version – myself, Jonathan and Hannah) would move to Grimsby and set up home there.

I grew dizzy trying to come up with a solution. We found a crumbling old house in Abbey Park Road, the old middle-class heart of Grimsby, close to the town centre, and applied for yet another mortgage. 1 Abbey Park Road was destined to remain a crumbling old house. For the decade we lived there it just crumbled more. Jack Straw (who was working with me at the time as a researcher on Granada's *World in Action*) had to give us advice on plastering the holes which kept appearing in the ceiling. We only had one car and I had not driven for years. Like most of the women of my generation, I accepted that if you had a family car, the man's place was in the driving seat.

In 1977 Britain had only recently achieved the Equal Pay Act. Equal opportunities for women – especially when it came to their family lives – were a distant dream, even at companies like Granada. I was working as a producer on *World in Action* and based in Manchester. Half the team were based in London. I asked my boss if I could work from London too. The answer was a definite no. In 1977 no one thought that women with children, who worked outside the home,

115

especially in well-paid middle-class jobs, deserved any special consideration. The opposite was often true and all too often women like myself accepted it. Like other trainee super-women of my generation, I believed that life was tough for women and those few who made it to the top did so because they were strong as well as smart. Women who had the education, got the husband and the kids had to demonstrate, *à la* Thatcher, that they could do everything.

Looking back, I see that we achieved very little by trying to do it all. We were women who adopted men's values. We won by taking men on on their terms. We spoke men's language. Of course we were sympathetic to our sisters stuck at home with the kids, but we thought of them as distant cousins. The women who were successful MPs and bringing up kids in the 1970s were a very small group: Margaret Thatcher herself, Gwyneth Dunwoody and Ann Taylor. Ann's children were at home in the north with her husband.

Ann Taylor: 'Some mornings when I came in and saw other mothers taking their kids to work, it used to be slightly poignant. I used to think, am I doing the right thing? I obviously never thought of it sufficiently to stop doing what I was doing, though, did I? But it has to be possible, otherwise you're excluding a whole range of women from being Members of Parliament.

'I kept them in the north and I travelled down. For the most part that worked reasonably well. I'd do the same again – partly because I don't want to bring up children in London and partly because when they're down here, there's always the pulling in two directions. Should you take them to lunch or do this bit of work or should you take them out somewhere or take them back to the flat? You end up doing work, but then they feel more miffed than if they were two hundred miles away. Because here they are and you're still not with them. So, yes, I would make the same decision, as long as I could feel secure enough about them.'

The late Bob Cryer, then the MP for Keighley and his wife Ann, who has now taken over his job, came to Grimsby to campaign for Austin in the Grimsby by-election. A few weeks later they invited us to their house in Oakworth for tea. We sat in their front room, which was dominated by two grey-steel filing cabinets full of Bob's constituency casework. Bob was utterly serious about his politics and Austin admired him. I was frightened by his dour Yorkshireness. Bob asked me about my work and how I managed with the twins. I gave a jaunty description of My Busy Life (I expect I thought it sounded extremely glamorous) which involved secret filming trips to South Africa and trouble with nannies and flying visits to the constituency. He said grimly that I had no business to be going out to work. I should be at home helping Austin to be a good MP and bringing up my kids. That was my real job. I never really forgave him, and I doubt he forgave me.

When I talked to his widow, Ann, who became Keighley's MP on 1 May, she said that it was not until just before Bob died, when Connor, his first grandchild arrived, that he realised how little time he had spent with his family and how much she had done alone. She had more or less brought up the children as a single mother while he 'worked'. In the 1990s he had begun to question whether he had been right to let her sacrifice her life for him and whether it had been right to weigh her and the kids down with living in the constituency.

Ann Cryer: 'He started to learn once Connor was born. Connor was eighteen months when Bob was killed. He started to ask all sorts of things like, "How did you manage?" "How did you manage with two of them, and me out all the time?" "I know I've been wrong, I know I've been wrong," he used to say. "I should have spent more time at home, but I was doing what I thought was right at the time and I know I – we've – made mistakes."

'He said he'd made two mistakes, he didn't spend enough time with the children and we shouldn't have lived in the constituency. When we moved away to Shipley, he said, "You know we should have done this when I was elected at first. We should have moved to Shipley. It would have just protected John and Jane."'

The problems of children who have to live with their parents' politics and often find themselves as the family ambassador in the constituency were mentioned by several Members. Dr Lynne Jones MP said that her son was 'very negative about it'. She had worked, right from when he was a baby, but becoming an MP seemed to be beyond the bounds of taste. 'He hates his friends knowing . . . I remember I had to give him a note for school and I did it on a plain piece of paper but I put it in a House of Commons envelope. He took it out of the envelope.'

Lynne Jones has strong family back-up when she is away in London. Her husband works locally and her mother is her childminder. Her other son Jack cheerfully accepts his mother's fame. 'At the school during the election campaign, one of the other lads said to Jack, "There's more pictures of your mum in King's Heath than the Spice Girls."'

Judith Church, who is separated from her husband, replaced Bryan Gould as the MP for Dagenham in 1994. She has a six-year-old and a nine-year-old. 'I manage because I have made certain decisions about a political career. Other than being an MP, I've decided I'm not going to attempt to be in office or to be in a major position on a Select Committee, or anything like that, because I try to get home to see the children, even if I've got to go back and vote in the evening at ten. I'm not going to be here all day and all evening and not get home to see them in the evenings. So I've made that choice – if you like – I mean I'm quite happy to be a backbench MP, doing things I'm interested in. When I first came here, I had the youngest children, and lots of people were saying to me, "Oh don't do what I did and never see your children." And I thought, well, I've no intention of doing that. Some people made that choice. And I don't think that it's a correct choice. I do think it's a very bizarre thing if we end up being governed by people who don't have a normal family life. Who are not in touch with what's going on in their children's schools on a daily basis – and you have to be with young children, you have to know what's going on with homework and, you know, discipline and problems at school. And you can't do that unless you're seeing them every evening.'

Politicians' offspring do have a tough time. Just at the age when they want to keep their parents a deep dark secret, Dad or Mum insists on being all over the front page of the local paper, talking about some stupid idea that everyone else in town disagrees with. In every newspaper picture from the 'photo opportunity' that launched the Blairs on their Italian summer holiday, the Prime Minister's sons Euan and Nicholas stared gloomily at the ground, while Tony and Cherie threw family-sized smiles to the photographers. On *The Moral Maze* there was serious discussion about how Euan Blair would cope when he was caught smoking his first cigarette. Who needs politicians for parents?

Janet Boateng: 'I think that some children do go through a hell of a lot of stress which parents aren't even aware of. People saying, "Oh your father wouldn't like that, would he?" or they go into their school and have a political discussion (my daughter's doing politics) and the teacher will say, "Oh, I hate all politicians" – in the presence of a child whose parent happens to be a Member of Parliament – so insensitive. "They can give themselves pay rises, and they think they are a law above everybody else." What do you feel if your child is sitting there listening to all of this?

'She gets a lot of flack. I don't really think people are aware of the sort of pain that the children sometimes have to go through. Even at the time when they said, "Paul Boateng sends his child to a grant-maintained school" – my child went to the school which I think was in her best interests. And that became a story in the press. She got followed by this journalist and she thought some strange man was following her and she ran off. The poor child was terrified.'

Some of the mums I spoke to were fiercely protective. Tess Kingham (Labour, Gloucester) did not want us filming her three-year-old in the Labour Party crêche at Brighton, and Harriet Harman was the only woman out of the ninety-two we interviewed who refused to answer any personal questions at all. 'I don't talk about family members because it invades their privacy, in my view,' she told us.

Claire Curtis-Thomas: 'Two or three weeks after I'd been elected, I brought the girls down. They went into the Royal

Gallery, which was great because they saw the Queen – they loved her hat, they told me afterwards, they just loved the hat. But by two o'clock in the afternoon we were all shattered and I sat my two children down with me in the Members' Lobby because they were really tired and my elder daughter Georgia's got a learning difficulty and she was exhausted. She was being really difficult and a policeman came up to me and said, "Excuse me, ma'am – you may sit, but your children may not." And he said, "They haven't been elected to sit here, you must take them somewhere else," and I thought that's really rather silly. Then I got told off because Georgia was jumping about, she has some behavioural difficulties, and I was told that I had to control her. I think it's pretty obvious that my daughter has a learning difficulty and I very much objected to the ignorance of the policeman who told me to try and control her.'

In a way Bob Cryer was right. A new MP needs all the help and support he or she can get. A spouse who takes on the job of family manager, who provides the children with a home life wherever that home might be, who protects the family from the outside world and allows the Member the freedom to go off to Westminster, and come home when business allows, is a jewel beyond price. And the MP is going to have a much easier time of it if she does not have to run the family as well.

Several female Members thought it was better to put off Westminster politics until the children were older. Llin Golding, for instance, thought it impossible to be a full-time mother as well as a full-time MP. 'You can't expect your colleagues to do your work for you when you go off and be a mother. That would cause a lot of resentment.' She agreed that it is especially hard if the kids are young, and there's no husband to provide support.

When Anne Campbell's children were younger, she would never have considered the idea of living away from home for three or four nights a week. But rather than her nursing some 'long-burning ambition' which she had to put off until her children were older, it was the opposite: 'Them being older put me in a position where I was able to consider it.'

When it comes to children, younger MPs like Oona King face a rather different problem. 'I want my Oona back the way she was before that fateful selection meeting,' her husband, Tiberio Santomarco, wrote movingly in the *Guardian*. 'I have to go to Westminster to dine with her, and if, at the end of the meal, I want to lean over and kiss her, I can't, because to kiss an MP might be seen as silly.' Too busy now, at the start of her parliamentary career, to spend more than one evening out of ten with her husband, will Oona ever have time to raise a family?

Oona King: 'I feel there is a huge pressure on me, even pressure from myself, not to have children now because I can't see how I would be able to enjoy them. On the other hand, my prospects don't look as though they are going to change that much [Bethnal Green and Bow being a very safe Labour seat] which means I will have to probably at some point have children as well as working in the House, and it is a very depressing scenario.'

In our family, it is accepted by all of us that we made a big mistake by going to live in the constituency. It was tough on the kids and tough on us. But it can be even tougher right at the top. In Gillian Slovo's book *Every Secret Thing* about her parents, Ruth First and Joe Slovo, Housing Minister in the South African coalition government, she describes the death of her father at his home in Johannesburg. It was the middle of the night and Nelson Mandela, her father's political leader and dear friend, came to pay his respects. 'The President looked across at us – Joe's daughters – sitting opposite and in the quietness of the day's dawning, he told a story. He told us how one day when he had gone to hug his grown-up daughter she had flinched away from him, and burst out, "You are the father to all our people, but you never had the time to be a father to me."'

Certainly, growing up as the child of an MP has a lot of disadvantages. And we discovered that many of Westminster's women were only coping thanks to tireless support from the wings.

7

MOTHERS OF PARLIAMENT

HALF OF THE 120 women who were elected to parliament on 1 May were brand-new Members. All had dreamed of their arrival at Westminster and most came with some sort of plan about how they would manage their family life; just the opposite of what Austin and I had done twenty years before. He had become an MP unexpectedly at a by-election, and our life became a hopeless muddle as we coped with what we could, when we could. These new Members seem much better organised and have often planned things in advance with their husbands and families.

Caroline Spelman, the only female MP with three children aged under seven, is the new Conservative Member for Meriden and one of the last candidates chosen for the general election. She replaced Ian Mills, who had been found dead in his London flat in April. Mills was middle-aged and lonely with a drink problem.

I drove to the Midlands to meet her. She and her husband Mark have rented a modern family house in a leafy street in Meriden. They had spent the afternoon at a village fête, not because Caroline was opening it, just because it was happening and they wanted to become part of constituency life. I didn't like to ask the question directly, but I got the impression that no one had recognised Caroline at the fête, and she, for her part, had not bothered to tell them she was their MP.

The Spelman family were crowded into the kitchen and Mark was getting the children's tea. Like kids all over Britain that Saturday afternoon, they were having fish fingers, chips and peas. The smallest child, a toddler called 'Pickle' by his parents, was cuddling his mum.

Caroline Spelman: 'Having quite young children represented quite a problem to a number of constituencies and I understand what those reservations were. I think Meriden was different in that respect – there it was regarded as an advantage to have a family.

'Obviously I didn't just spring this upon Mark. He knew I wanted to go into politics before we got married, so we've grown up to it together and we were together when I fought my last seat, so he had practical experience of what was involved. I had my first child during the time that I fought Bassetlaw, so we were able to work out how, as young parents, we would manage the family responsibilities, as well as nursing the seat, so that both fronts were looked after.

'I can remember having a conversation and saying – right, now this is how it's going to work. All along the line, he and I have talked it through. It's very important to look at the practical implications. This seat, for example, has very good communications to London. There are two trains an hour, it only takes an hour and twenty-five minutes, all of which helps us manage the two bases. It's not just me "doing politics", regardless of everybody else – we've got to look at it as a complete picture with everybody's needs taken care of.'

Caroline's children are six, four and two. They had rather unconventional ideas about what her new job entailed . . .

'My four year old thinks I've gone to work at Big Ben. Just to correct a few false impressions, fairly early on I took them up to the House with me, and with my secretary, who knows the place better than I do, we walked through the two Chambers together, and I showed them where I sit. And they can relate that bit better now to what they see on the television. Coming back from the Lords, which is of course very ornate, my six-year-old daughter said, "Oh it's a bit plain in here, Mummy." On the day of the Queen's Speech, I couldn't take them to school because things were starting a bit earlier. I was trying to explain to my youngest that I was going to see the Queen and all he could say was, "I want to go and talk to the Queen."'

Mark Spelman is determined that he and Caroline will both have opportunities to develop their careers: 'I think the great thing you have to do when you've opted for two careers is to recognise that there are times when different priorities become more important. Supporting Caroline, I learnt the importance of flexibility: one minute you might be having a meeting in the boardroom and the next minute you might be in Tesco's or changing the kids' clothes.'

Mark and Caroline have decided to move their family home from Maidenhead to Meriden. They want the children to have a stable base and they have decided that Caroline will do the travelling. Mark and the children will move to the constituency, and they will continue to have a full-time nanny.

Caroline Spelman: 'As far as I'm concerned, physical location is less of an important issue because I travel quite a bit in my job. It's very important to be based in the constituency so I feel it's absolutely the right thing to move and to be based here.'

Mark cheerfully accepts that he is at the vanguard of modern marriage. 'A lot of my male friends are quite challenged by Caroline. I think one of the secrets of our success is that by having two careers which are both moving forward fairly rapidly, we challenge and excite one another and I think there's a vibrancy in our relationship. Where I work, the husbands tend to have the careers and the wives tend to support them. But everybody has to find out what works for them. I'm totally behind her because I think she's very good at it, so my role is to give her every chance of being successful.'

Caroline Spelman: 'It requires lots of give and take on both sides. I think that's actually very good, there's a lot of sparkle that emanates from that. I mean you really appreciate, as a woman, if your husband is prepared to sacrifice things for you.'

What distinguishes the family life of the new female MPs is their cheerful acceptance of complicated arrangements, balancing kids, spouse, constituencies and work at Westminster.

Sandra Osborne has a thirteen-year-old daughter at home with her husband: 'I phone them every night. I still have to keep tabs, especially on what my youngest daughter's doing, and just remind her about things. Just the same as if I was up there. I think it's important she's aware that although I'm not there, I'm thinking about her here. I go up every weekend and they can and do come down. But of course that's constrained by school and work. But it was important just to show Emma that this is what I do, this is where I am, this is where my office is, this is where I sleep.'

Liz Blackman also spends a lot of time on the phone – several times a day. She feels confident that, in spite of the upheavals, her family has adapted to her new job. 'They've got their own lives mapped out for them at the moment. We weren't seeing much of each other during the working week when I was at home, but even if they hadn't seen me all day and I'd been to a council meeting in the evening, they would know I was in my bed and they would see me in the morning. And of course that's different now.'

Beverley Hughes: 'My youngest son, Michael, has missed me quite a lot and was actually – I didn't realise it was this until a few weeks in – quite worried about me. He would say on the phone, "Where are you?" and, "Oh, you're not on your own are you, Mummy? Is there anyone with you? Are you all right?" It was helpful when he came down, about three weeks ago, and brought me furniture and stuff and got a mental picture of where I was. I think he still does miss me, I try to ring him once a day.'

Anne McGuire's children are twenty-one and nineteen and live at home.

Anne McGuire: 'It's strange to be back into a house where you haven't been for four days and finding not just that life goes on without you but that they buy different things for the cupboard. We've always shared the shopping, but it used to be my shopping agenda, if you want to put it that way. I decided when we had cream of mushroom soup or tomato.'

Helen Brinton's children are exactly the ages (Hal is fifteen, Gwendoline twelve) when a mother can be an embarrassment if she steps out of line. 'They've been horrified by it really,' she admits. 'They're at that stage where it's been embarrassing, because I'm doing things that other mums aren't doing.' She recalls when she was first standing in Faversham. 'There had to be a big fight to get them to even appear as a family group on the election address.' This time, she confesses, she didn't even bother to ask the question, and her children didn't come to Peterborough once.

But Patricia Hewitt's children feel that they see more of her now she is an MP. 'About three weeks after the election, my daughter, who is ten, said to me, "It's much nicer you being an MP, Mum, than when you were at Anderson's." I've been in the private sector for the last two and a half years and, plus being a candidate or trying to become a candidate, it's been a bit of a nightmare. I've been heading off to work at eight or eight-thirty every morning, never managing to take the children to school. Then the first few weeks after the election I was taking them to school every day, as we didn't have any-one living in at that point and I was making their school lunches and dropping them off and we really loved it. We do see much more of each other now because I've got one occu-pation instead of having a full-time job and being a candidate – I'm used to trying to juggle, not always successfully, all the different bits.

'The problem with being an MP, as I expected, is the late nights. Up until now one of us has generally been home by seven o'clock every evening and maybe both of us out one night a week. We'll just see how the voting and the whipping system settles down.'

When Peckham CLP selected her for the 1983 general elec-tion, Harriet Harman seemed like just another ordinary prospective candidate. But in 1982, when the incumbent, Larry Lambourne died, she was pregnant. 'I remember think-ing at the time they would be on the phone saying – now you're pregnant you can't stand. I thought that, having selected me not pregnant, they'd expect me to get elected the same way. But because I've got such a strong record and had been part of a strong movement of campaigning for women's rights, I think nobody dared ring me up. People might have thought it, but nobody said it.'

Ruth Kelly became a mother four weeks after she became an MP. She managed to fit in her maiden speech before she went off to produce Eammon.

Ruth Kelly: 'I was selected on Mother's Day last year, in March, and I was named on 1 June, so you can imagine all the preparations that had to take place. Having Derek, my husband, helping me was a huge asset over the course of the next year. Eammon was born on 26 May this year. I have ideas about the future I'd like for myself but precisely how they're carried out and done and in what ways, I leave open to fate. I wanted a family young. A lot of people said to me, "Gosh aren't you going to find this hard?" I mean talk about bad timing, being pregnant during the campaign, and I was saying to myself: "Well, it's going to be difficult, but then, if you're going to have a family and you're a politician, there's never going to be a good time." In the course of my career or the course of my time as an MP, I hope to be building up responsibilities, not shedding them. Having a family young is great and we're both delighted.'

Sally Keeble has two small children, a three-year-old and a toddler of eighteen months. She and her husband have had a house in south London since they were married and about six months after she had been selected they bought a place in Northampton. They live in London from Monday to Thursday and on Friday she takes the children up to the constituency for the weekend. Her husband gets the train up after work on Friday. But she admits it is a hassle, particularly in terms of cost. 'I have a nanny down here, and then in Northampton my husband looks after them or there's a babysitting agency that I use there as well. It's expensive, very expensive – probably getting on for half my net salary.'

One way that new women Members cope is to create a small business with the husband/partner acting as secretary/organiser, and if there are children the childcare is juggled between the couple: a neat role reversal of the old-style parliamentary couple and the 1997 version of the way Labour

Members and their wives ran their constituencies in the 1970s and 1980s. When Bryan Gould was the MP for Dagenham, his wife Gill was always at his side, notebook at the ready, as well as being mother to their kids Charles and Helen.

The new women Members have a famous role model at the Palace. The President of the Board of Trade, Margaret Beckett and her husband Leo have been working together at Westminster (without kids to bring up) since she became MP for Derby South in 1983.

Margaret Beckett: 'He had always been a volunteer Party worker, and it was nearly as much part of his life as it is for most MPs, and so we went on working together. He was a house husband for two or three years while I was out of parliament. Then when I came back, because he'd always been the constituency liaison person, or one of the key constituency liaison people for a string of MPs, it seemed the obvious thing for him to come and set up the liaison for the new constituency. So he came down to London to sort out our accommodation and to help establish the constituency links. It just worked and it's gone on working, and so he's gone on managing my office. We are very fortunate because our working life is around the House of Commons and the Department, and is very much shared . . . we are both political activists and always have been together. Leo tells a story from fairly early on, about one of the women police officers, funnily enough, on duty at the Members' Entrance. Leo and I arrived there together, and I went walking on towards the cloakroom and she said to Leo, "Where does that lady think she's going?" And Leo had to explain that I was actually the Member of Parliament. A male policeman who used to be on the gate, stopped us several times, and said, "Now let me get this straight – she's the MP and you're the spouse?"'

Caroline Flint has three children and a partner, Phil Cole. Phil was a PR executive at Burston Marsteller, and gave it up to work as Caroline's assistant. They share the childcare, but the majority of the responsibility falls on him.

Caroline Flint: 'Phil always wanted me to be an MP. I know that might sound quite strange, and people ask me – since I've become an MP – "When's Phil going for it?" So I have to say, and Phil would say it himself: "There's enough men." I know it sounds terribly "new man" but he's been wonderful – he's always been interested in politics, and politically active, but being an MP hasn't been something he's wanted to do, and he's supported me one hundred per cent.

'We were conscious of me wanting to be a good constituency MP, and also conscious of our family life. With Phil working for me, not only does it enable me to do a good job in terms of the constituency . . . but also with the family as well. Whilst I am obviously going to have to work long hours and it will take up chunks of the weekend, there's a parent there. We've just swapped these roles round. I'm learning to adjust, to trust Phil, that he'll keep all the lists in his head about packed lunches, sport today, etc. I'm sure we're going to have a few mistakes on the way, but it's sharing a lot more and it's . . . very liberating.'

Jacqui Smith's husband looks after their three-year-old son and runs her constituency office. She describes their son as being 'reasonably disinterested in the whole thing'. Recently, she brought him up to have a look round the House of Commons. 'He enjoyed going into the Chamber, "Where you have the meetings, Mummy", although I think he enjoyed more going down to Whitehall and looking at the Horse Guards.'

Her political career could not have taken off without a team effort. When her husband was made redundant a few years ago he didn't take another job, but stayed at home to look after their child and to provide back-up and support for Jacqui. He helped as a campaign co-ordinator during the election and is now working for her in the constituency. 'It puts pressures on as well,' she admits, 'if you're both obviously dependent on the one job and the same success, but at least it means I can talk to him.' Not that the dream team are free from their share of problems, though. 'It's very important that you make a distinction between when you're talking in relation to work and when you're talking in relation to family – we don't always succeed. On top of all that . . . you're apart for four days a week and you've got to deal with that.'

Kali Mountford: 'It was our wedding anniversary this week and obviously I was here and he was there, we hardly spoke about it. We did try and talk but when we did, it was, "Have you heard from such and such about this case? Have you arranged that meeting?" It was all work. And it's my fault. I can't, I don't switch off very much.'

The majority of women MPs do not have any childcare responsibilities. Only a few have children under five. Twenty-two per cent have children between 5 and 15, 65 per cent are married, 5 per cent divorced and 17 per cent single.

'Supportive' and 'I could never have made it without him' are terms used by most of the married women about their husbands.

Eleanor Laing: 'He's been very supportive and we've moved to the constituency. It's not very convenient, but it's not too bad for him. He enjoys the constituency side . . . meeting people in the area. We've got a lot of very rich people and we go to a lot of social events which are very pleasant. He's an international businessman and a lawyer. He does have an interest in politics and economics, but very much from a business point of view. That's good for me, it means I get a constant input of what the business world is thinking about our policies. I think there is a danger that politicians become insulated from the outside world and they don't realise how their decisions or their outlook are affecting the business world. After all, unless business is working, they're not creating jobs and they're not creating prosperity, so that's very important.'

Valerie Davey's husband is the only one we found who actually supports and stands for a different Party.

Valerie Davey: 'He is in fact a member of the Green Party. He would have much preferred a different government and a different approach. So he's finding it just as he did when I was on the county council: something I do, something that I find valuable and therefore he accepts it, rather than being involved in it. He has, over the years, stood in the local elections, and is usually agent for the Green Party in the general election. We know where we're coming from, we know what we think. It's very useful always to be questioning what you're doing. There's always a recognition at home that there's a different point of view.'

Laura Moffatt's husband has a guilty secret: 'He's very embarrassed but he's actually voted Tory once in his life. But then he came from a Tory family.'

Linda Perham's husband made a wonderful Mayoress to her Mayor, while he was working full-time as director of engineering for the Metropolitan Police. He even managed to run the charity committees, a task normally taken on by a retired lady. His support, she says, is personal, not political. 'He's tremendously supportive and not at all political. He thinks politics are a bit of a joke really but he supports me personally.'

Janet Anderson: 'I was very much in favour of Sunday shopping, and I was one of the first people to stick my neck out, and I remember in a debate in the House standing up and saying, "It's not that my husband is unwilling to do the shopping, it's just that when he does, he generally gets it wrong." And of course they repeated this on *Yesterday in Parliament* the following day and he was absolutely furious. Well it's true, he never gets the kind of crisps the kids like. Even if you write it on the list quite clearly.'

Candy Atherton and Lorna Fitzsimons both live with parents. Candy Atherton has lived with her 75-year-old father, an ex-*Mirror* journalist, for several years. 'I have some caring responsibilities. But I don't have children. I think it would be very, very difficult to have young children and be representing a constituency as far away as mine.'

Lorna Fitzsimons: 'I have a mum and she's brill. I live with her in the constituency. You do wonder when you're ever going to leave yourself time to do the things like find a partner and get married and have kids, but they will come with time.'

There is one new category of Members in this parliament: the women who declare openly that they are living with a man to whom they are not married, and bringing up kids who could be hers, his or theirs. Caroline Flint, Jane Griffiths and Melanie Johnson are all in this group. Melanie Johnson received national attention from the press during the election campaign when the sitting Conservative MP for her constituency, David Evans, called her children 'bastards'. (It made no difference to the voters: there was a swing to Labour of 11.05 per cent in Welwyn Hatfield.)

The freedom to have an unconventional private life and still win the voters was an important change in this parliament. Only eighteen years ago, Labour's new Public Health Minister Tessa Jowell first stood for parliament in 1979 in the Ilford North by-election. She was maligned in the press for a lifestyle which would today be regarded as normal. In 1979 she was a 32-year-old psychiatric social worker, a voluntary sector worker and London Labour councillor. She had left her first husband Roger Jowell and was living with banker David Mills. It was a bitter by-election because the newspapers found out about her unconventional home life, the National Front were active and so was the Society for the Protection of the Unborn Child.

Tessa Jowell: 'I remember when I came back after having been selected and David said the *Daily Mail* had been on the phone. And they had apparently said to him, "We want to talk to Tessa Jowell," and he said, "She's not back yet." This voice at the end of the phone said, "Are you her father?" And he said, "No, no, I live here." That was how the whole thing started to run. And it was absolutely ghastly. I remember one of the worst moments was when one Labour supporting newspaper said, "We'll do a sympathetic story." The next morning it appeared under the heading, with my photograph with my head thrown back coquettishly – Live Confessions of Labour's Tessa. I just thought, "I can never get out of bed again."

'The thing about going through this, having them camping on your doorstep and all the rest of it, is that it does become defining: you feel as you've got the black spot for ever and that nobody actually ever thinks about you in any other terms other than as this woman who was living with a married man. It does terrible things to your ability to trust people.'

There are strong feelings among the new women at

Westminster that their private lives are their own affair and nothing to do with the press or their constituents.

Melanie Johnson: 'I've got twin daughters who are thirteen and a son who's ten and the girls are getting to that age where they're growing increasingly independent. It's more difficult for my son because he's that bit younger. But they'll all be at secondary school next year. My partner's parents live round the corner from us and they do quite a lot of the early morning and early evening childcare and my partner tries to get home early a couple of nights a week in order to look after them from six o'clock onwards.

'My partner's been pretty good about my political life all told. He's not a political animal himself.'

Caroline Flint says she did worry about the people of Don Valley and what they would make of the fact that she is not married to her partner, Phil Coles, with whom she is bringing up three children (two hers, one his) from former marriages. But the people of Don Valley cheerfully accepted her even after the local paper described her as 'unmarried mother of three'. Caroline and Phil are still nervously careful to make the situation super-clear to everyone. At a *Vogue* photo-shoot featuring men who work for their wives, Caroline and Phil were cuddling up to one another as directed. 'Look into your husband's eyes, darling,' called the photographer. 'He's not my husband,' called back Caroline determinedly.

Jane Griffiths: 'I can't think of any reason why it should matter. In the Tory government there was all this stuff about family values, but most of the people weren't living by that themselves, even if they were married. Society's changed, things have moved on.'

If we put on one side the damage to the family which can be caused by a press campaign, it is the Members with childcare responsibilities who face the toughest choices. Members live in two and sometimes three places and have to accept that unless they have London constituencies, they will have to spend at least part of the week separated from their families.

It is interesting that in those families where the husband or partner does not have his own career, or is prepared to give up his career, or forgo promotion to help his partner, he often plays a key role in childcare arrangements. The fact that the House of Commons Secretarial Allowance can be used to pay a husband or partner who acts as secretary or office manager as well as childcare provider is regarded as a bonus. In this parliament, very few female Members with small children have husbands who are high flyers. Those who do, rely on professional childcare. Caroline Spelman, Sally Keeble and Karen Buck all have full-time nannies and other halves with flourishing careers.

Quite a number of Members get help from other family members. Ruth Kelly's parents live near her and help with Eammon. Melanie Johnson gets help from her partner's parents. Clare Curtis-Thomas's twin sister looks after her daughters when she is at Westminster. Lynne Jones relies on her mother.

But most female Members do not have childcare responsibilities: the average age of women Members is forty-five and many have grown-up children, or no children at all. Parliamentary partners are important in this category. Margaret Beckett, President of the Board of Trade and her husband and office manager Leo, are the government's best-known Westminster couple, and a shining role model for new Members.

In the evenings, when the office staff go home, the Commons becomes much more like its famous designation as 'the best club in London' and couples are seen eating together in the restaurants or sharing a drink on the Terrace, which overlooks the Thames. For as long as I can remember, Margaret and Leo have been sharing a table in the cafeteria, quietly talking over their day together like a contented couple in their own front room. Alice Mahon (Labour, Halifax) and her husband Tommy are also a Westminster item. They arrive together in the morning. He opens her post and then goes off happily to spend an hour in the staff canteen, which is always packed with hungry policemen queuing for full English breakfasts and mountains of baked beans on toast.

These older political couples are the ones who seem to have

adapted best to Westminster life. They have someone to go home to at the end of the day, a travelling companion for those endless trips to the constituency. It can be a lonely, itinerant life for the women Members without husbands or partners, and it is a constant juggling act on a giant scale for those with childcare responsibilities.

8

VOTES FOR THE GIRLS

THE ELECTION OF 120 women to the House of Commons was greeted with delight by newspapers, voters and politicians of every hue. 'Never before have women been so well represented in parliament, and even though some of them are there thanks to a quota system, that must be a cause for celebration', trumpeted an editorial in the *Daily Mail*.

'It's fantastic,' said Helen Jackson, Labour MP for Sheffield Hillsborough since 1992. The week after the election she was struck by the way people in the street, in the shops, the checkouts in supermarkets came up to her and said, 'it must be great having all those women there.' Marion Roe, MP for Broxbourne since 1983, agreed: 'Taking my Conservative hat off, I thought – about time, too.'

But there are sceptics too, mostly Conservatives, who maintain that gender is irrelevant in politics and should stay that way. It took Ann Widdecombe three general elections to win herself a seat, but she never blamed that on being a woman. Quite the contrary: 'I always used to sell it very positively. I used to say anything you do as a woman is twice as noticeable.' Did she feel pleased to see more women in parliament? 'What I've always said is that I want a meritocracy. If we happen to have 650 women or 650 men it doesn't matter so long as what we've got is the 650 most able people that were on offer.'

Newcomer Theresa May agrees: 'I don't think in terms of the role of women in politics as such. I mean I think that we should aim to have 659 good Members of Parliament, regardless of whether they're male or female.' I put a similar question to Ann Winterton. If she could have a parliament full of 659 very competent MPs would she like 300 of them to be women? 'No I wouldn't. I don't believe in this so-called equal representation thing. I'm elected to serve the electorate in Congleton – men, women and children. I believe that the electorate are more important, in this matter, than somebody sitting up on high and saying, "We'll have 300 of each." Quite wrong.'

And of course they do have a point. Constituencies are defined by geography, not gender, after all, and in theory a woman MP is just as capable of neglecting the interests of the opposite sex as a man.

What is necessarily so great about having 120, or 300, or 330, women MPs? Simple, according to Clare Short: 'Increasing women's representation in Parliament is essential if we are to build a House of Commons which more truly represents the whole population. As more women come into the Commons, the culture will change, the agenda of politics will broaden, and the institution itself will be transformed.'

Cheryl Gillan agrees. This is a question of proper representation: 'We do need more women in politics, after all we're fifty-two per cent of the population and we are representatives not delegates and if you're going to be representative then you must have a certain proportion of women within the legislative.' Gillian Shephard thought it was 'marvellous' that so many women got in. 'I've listened to some of their maiden speeches, and on my own side as well, and what is so clear is that they come with a huge variety of backgrounds. Now that, ultimately, is going to enrich the House and enrich government.'

In the end even Ann Widdecombe admitted, 'When people sit and look and see a lot of Labour women and not very many Conservative women, they will think to themselves this is something to be redressed and that will be in the back of their minds as they go through selections . . .' And Theresa May contradicted herself, confessing that she was 'interested in trying to encourage more Conservative women to come forward to be on the list'. Though none of the Conservatives I spoke to said they had supported Labour's policy of all-women shortlists, the overwhelming consensus of opinion was that more women MPs were a cause for celebration.

And on a sunny Saturday in July, ten weeks into the new government, 600 women came to the Labour Party's women's training conference in Bournemouth to do just that. Old MPs, new MPs, wannabe MPs in trouser-suits and mini-skirts and floral-print dresses. There were CLP delegates by the bus-load. Junior Ministers, Cabinet Ministers, the Minister for Women. Everyone was there, even Tony Blair, who came to fill the 'Key Note Address: Speaker to be confirmed' slot just before lunch. Some were disappointed that he only managed to mention the woman word once, but we shuffled from the darkened auditorium on high moral ground, swooning with promises and good intentions all the same. Outside Margaret Prosser stood with a TGWU minibus-load of reps with clip-boards, gathering petitions for the BA dispute. I spotted Linda Perham chatting with friends in the queue outside Harry Ramsden's fish and chip shop. Three young girls in dazzling white trainers strolled along the edge of the beach swigging alcopops.

Joan Ruddock chaired the afternoon session and Mo Mowlam spoke first, taking questions from the floor on the subject of women in Northern Ireland. Even the journalists got to their feet to clap. We had been warned she had to go early because the marching season wasn't over yet, but for a moment she seemed reluctant to leave. Joan gave her a kiss and a hug goodbye as the Secretary of State for International Development stepped up to the mike to give the final key-note speech.

'Do you remember when everyone was complaining about all-women shortlists?' Clare Short said. Everyone laughed. 'Do you remember when I said how it might be. We'd be sitting in the House of Commons, on the other side. And there'd be all these women of different ages, different backgrounds and colours transforming the image of the place and bringing a transformation into the institution of parliament?' A mur-

138

mur went round the auditorium. 'And I said that when it happens, everyone will pretend they were always in favour.' More laughter. Clare paused, nearly fluffing the punch-line. 'We did it, and they are pretending.'

Later I asked her how it had felt sitting in the House for the first time after 1 May, when everyone crowded in to swear the Oath of Allegiance and re-elect the Speaker. 'I tried to describe it to people in my speeches,' she said, 'when people were feeling worried about the all-women shortlists, so I had the picture in my mind quite clearly, and it wasn't just like seeing: I knew it, and there it was, so I wasn't really surprised. I knew they were coming. I knew it would look different. I knew it would be nicer, and it was . . .'

So much nicer that everybody seems to want to be an MP now. As holiday-makers smoothed their towels on Bournemouth's powdery yellow sand and wondered whether to go for a Sunday dip, conference delegates faced an even tougher choice: which skills workshop should they attend? There were eighteen in all, ranging from 'Building a Woman-Friendly Party', to 'Speaking up in Public', and 'Running Local Campaigns'. Or how about 'Getting Your Message Across Through the Media'? Or 'Standing for the Welsh Assembly or Scottish Parliament'? Unable to contain my curiosity, I decided to give 'Standing as an MP' a go, and rushed up-hill to the Swallow International Hotel's Poole Room, where Helen Jackson and new Enfield North MP Joan Ryan had already started expounding upon the four Cs (Cash, Childcare, Culture and Confidence) to a group of twenty or thirty hopefuls. According to Labour Women's Network, Emily's List, the Liberal Democrat Party, the Fawcett Society and countless other such organisations, these four Cs are what have been keeping large numbers of women away from Westminster for the last seventy-odd years.

What the hopefuls hadn't yet realised, of course, was that Labour probably won't manage to get more than another ten to fifteen women into parliament in the next ten years, and that's if things go well. For the serious wannabes, Bournemouth was a waste of money. For anyone with real political ambition, now is surely the perfect time to turn Conservative.

As the discussion degenerated into a question-and-answer session of excruciatingly detailed irrelevance, it soon became apparent that none of these women were likely to appear in the parliament of 2002, or 2006 for that matter. How many years did you have to be a Party member before you could stand as a candidate? one of them wanted to know. Was it best to get your CV printed professionally or would a photocopy do? Listening to them I couldn't help wondering whether a similar group of men would have sat through such a wasted hour without complaint. Still, the political parties will never get more women to think seriously about politics if they're only prepared to talk to the ones who behave like men. At this stage, quality is irrelevant, the only important qualification is having the guts to stand up and say you're interested.

Ever since the publication of the Women's Election Committee pamphlet *See How They Grow!* in 1923 people have been campaigning to get more women into parliament. According to another leaflet of the period 1,057,425 votes had been cast for women candidates since 1918. 'PLEASE BRING THESE FACTS TO THE ATTENTION OF THE LOCAL CHAIRMAN OF YOUR PARTY' it concluded. As early as 1927 the women's section of the Labour Party conference was suggesting that every constituency party make an annual donation to a national fund for the support of women candidates.

In spite of this, the numbers returned did not grow steadily. Political parties only tended to entrust women candidates with marginal, or unwinnable, seats and this meant women MPs were vulnerable to even the slightest voting shifts. After the general election of 1979 the number of women MPs was lower than it had been in 1945. By the 1980s people were beginning to realise that simple 'encouragement' was not enough.

Tipped off by the 36-year-old Parliamentary Under-Secretary of State for the Environment, Angela Eagle MP, I arranged to meet Maureen Rooney, National Women's Officer of the Amalgamated Engineering and Electrical Union

(AEEU). A twenty-minute train ride south from Victoria took me deep into the heart of Bromley. It seemed an odd place for the headquarters of a union with 750,000 members, but the 140 AEEU employees working there are proud of Hayes Court and rightly so. The seventeenth-century former mansion, hospital and girls' school sprawls in several acres of neatly mown garden with, as Rooney's secretary confided, plenty of room left over for parking spaces. When I arrived the rain had just stopped and a tea-trolley was going round. The atmosphere was friendly and informal. Rooney directed me to a comfy chair and clipped the microphone to her blouse. I was there to ask about Labour's policy of all-women shortlists, but what could a trade union with a membership of only 10 per cent women have had to do with it?

'We were very much proactive in the changes that came about, the selection of Members of Parliament,' she said. In a way it all goes back to the Party conference of 1984, when Neil Kinnock tried to win support for his programme of modernisation.

According to his former researcher who is now MP for Leicester West, Patricia Hewitt, Kinnock 'would have liked to go for the Electoral College system and a much stronger element of one member one vote right from the outset', including some form of quota system in favour of women. A number of Party members supported the policy, but in 1984 they knew they wouldn't be able to get it through conference. The policy was too strongly identified with people from the Women's Action Committee and die-hard women's conference supporters. 'I think it's the old story of not paying attention to the message but who the messenger was,' said Rooney. 'What they were saying was probably quite fair, but how they were going about it probably antagonised people.' A case of poor presentation then.

After Rooney, I went to see the former National Officer for Equality at Manufacturing, Science and Finance (MSF). It was lunchtime. A receptionist directed me past a line of blown-up photographs of Tony Blair opening the union's newly renovated Islington office block to the lift. Anne Gibson sat at a cluttered desk in her office, stirring a cup-a-soup. I asked her what had happened in 1984. 'I think it was the view of many of us that we'd got as far as we could in actually just asking for equal rights for women in particular without some kind of back-up . . . we needed something within the Labour Party to really place us on the map as the Party that actually did care about equality.' The more they talked about it, the more obvious it became that one of the things they should try for was quotas 'because we couldn't rely just on good will'.

Rooney had said the resolution failed because the Women's Action Committee was regarded as being too extreme, but Gibson saw darker forces in play. 'There was a backlash because what you're actually talking about is power, and nobody likes to give up power lightly. It's all right when it's just the girls talking and having their own little conference and it doesn't come into the mainstream, but once it actually begins to percolate into the mainstream, the boys and some of the girls don't want their power dissipated.'

Margaret Prosser, then Women's Officer at the Transport and General Workers' Union (TGWU), agreed. 'There were a lot of men in the trade unions who didn't want to see any of this happening, and I think part of that was because they saw the women who were struggling for it as being women who were not in their control.' It was a power struggle? 'Oh yes, very much so.' 'We knew there'd be a battle,' said Gibson cheerfully, sipping her lunch.

Several battles in fact, on several fronts. Round one: the women's conference itself. Organisation is the key to effective political lobbying, and in the early 1980s the Labour Party's women's organisation was a complete and utter shambles. According to Maureen O'Mara, former National Women's Officer for the National Union of Public Employees (NUPE), the women's conference 'had no credence, really, within the movement at all. Within the Party, people regarded it as a joke, you know, and therefore those of us who went along to it were regarded as a joke.'

Gibson agreed: 'The women's conference was a laugh in the Party . . . you mentioned that you were going to the Labour

Party women's conference and there was a hoot of laughter and "Can't you think of anything better to do?"' The first time Rooney attended, she told me, it was 'an awakening experience, it was a wild conference'. A far cry from the Bournemouth training conference, 1997, then? Absolutely, said Gibson. 'They weren't just wild, they were totally bonkers some of them.'

I asked her what she meant by that, exactly. 'I remember years ago being at Newcastle for the women's conference of the NEC,' she told me. 'At that time there were men, some men on the NEC women's committee, and as soon as they appeared on the platform it was "Off, Off, Off". Even the people who were working behind the scenes, some of whom were men, were shouted off. And the atmosphere was horrendous. A lot of intimidation, to women speakers as well as to men, if you didn't tow the mili line . . . when people like Larry Whitty attended, they got howled down . . . it was just becoming anarchic.' If something hadn't been done, she concluded, they'd have had to close it down. 'The more it got a bad name, the more people like the general secretaries of unions said, "No, we can't justify sending a whole group of women."'

The conference and the women attending it lost all credibility. According to Prosser, it had been members of the Women's Action Committee who first put equality issues on the political agenda, back in the 1960s, but now their demands and resolutions were politically naïve, implausible. This was not all the responsibility of the hard-left women in Militant Tendency, however. It would never have got so bad, if only the NEC had taken the Women's Organisation seriously in the first place.

'They didn't put sufficient resources into the women's conference. They didn't plan for it in a proper way and so it began to be taken over and became completely irrelevant to the rest of the debate . . . Most of them, I think . . . saw women as being completely irrelevant.'

By any account this was a big mistake. In the 1980s the size and composition of Britain's workforce underwent radical changes. Margaret Thatcher had been doing her worst in engineering. The TGWU was losing members hand over fist. Rooney's union, the AEEU, lost something like a million jobs, most of them in the heavy, traditionally 'male' sector. Gibson's union, MSF, went through the same experience. 'I'm using very black and white terms here, but men's work going down and women's work going up – there are grey areas – but that's what's been happening.' And on top of that more workers were being employed part-time. 'You add all that together,' said Prosser, with a rueful smile, 'and the trade union movement decided it had better start recruiting women.' Even in NUPE, a female union, although the people running it tended to be men, they knew they had to change. 'If you were saying you were responsive to the needs of women, in the Eighties and the Nineties, you got a lot of Brownie points,' O'Mara told me.

Of course politicians and union leaders alike had been claiming sympathy with the cause of women workers for years, the difference now was that the unions (and the Labour Party itself, some would argue) were fighting for survival. As Prosser explained, 'There was a huge drop in membership, a recognition that you had to encourage women to become involved in order to, kind of, increase the membership, keep the union viable. In order to do that you had to present an image of your organisation as something that was halfway friendly towards women. So to be trying to do that on the one hand, and then standing up on [Party] conference floor and arguing against women's involvement on the other became an untenable position.' More or less reluctantly the movement reconciled itself to change. And with this came a growing confidence on the part of male trade unionists in their senior women officials.

Empowered by these developments, the trades union women decided it was time to tackle the women's conference. A number of them got together and took it by the scruff of the neck. 'We had to turn it into a body that was serious and more reasonable and pragmatic about things,' said O'Mara. She sat calmly, poised on the edge of a conference table, looking me straight in the eye. 'And how we did that, of course, was by changing the voting rules.'

At the stormy Island of Bute conference in 1986, they introduced an electoral college in which the trade unions and the Constituency Labour Parties each had 50 per cent of the vote and then proceeded to systematically vote down every remaining militant resolution. Angela Eagle called twenty-three card votes herself. 'I was threatened and spat at on several occasions, earning a special mention in *Militant* for my pain,' she remembers.

A tripartite committee, made up of CLP members, NEC members and members from the trade union side, was set up to run the women's organisation, and then they got down to some serious discussion.

Meanwhile, the psephologists had discovered an interesting statistical blip to chuck into the debate. The results of the 1983 general election revealed a striking difference in the voting patterns of men and women. According to this 'gender gap', women were 8 per cent more likely to vote Conservative than men. A perplexing discovery since, traditionally, women voters were thought more likely to share and respond to Labour's values than men. During the 1987 election campaign, the gap appeared to close, but the catch-up proved temporary. By April 1990 the polls revealed that women were once again less likely to vote Labour than men.

In 1989 a study by Labour's Shadow Communication Agency confirmed these findings. The evidence was presented to the Shadow Cabinet and the NEC. Almost simultaneously, the Parliamentary Labour Party (PLP) voted to support a proposal for a limited quota system designed to get more women elected to the Shadow Cabinet. That same year conference passed Composite 54 by a two-thirds majority. It committed the Party to introduce quotas of 40 per cent for elections at every level, and to achieve 50 per cent representation of women in the parliamentary Party in ten years or after three elections. Even so, by 1992 the gender gap had widened to a stage where women were 8 percentage points less likely to vote for Labour than men. It lost Labour the election.

At this stage, women MPs, people from the NEC Women's Committee, and the trades union movement had been pressing for quotas for years. When the gender gap came back after 1987, all of a sudden everybody seemed to think quotas were a good idea. So was the policy supported as a cynical attempt to win more votes in the 1992 election and then again, after 1992, in 1997?

I put the question to Deborah Lincoln, former National Women's Officer of the Labour Party. She works for the Prince's Trust now, but told me her attic is still stuffed with papers and cuttings relating to her days at Walworth Road. 'I'm not sure whether cynicism's quite fair. I think the Party had genuinely not allowed itself to think that there was such a gender gap,' she said. She did not think those at the top had actually realised there was a huge problem. O'Mara agreed. People 'were committed to the cause of women, they were feminists. They wanted the Party to move on these issues too.'

According to Prosser, the gender gap was just 'another influential factor. Nothing happens in isolation, does it? All of these things are interrelated, and the effect of the work done in the Sixties by the feminist movement, the change in the nature of the labour market, the demographic timebomb that we were all so worried about – there not being enough schoolboys leaving to fill all these jobs, and so suddenly childcare hit the home pages of the *Guardian*, rather than the women's page. All of that was a reflection that women in society were changing.'

Even so, Lincoln admitted that finding out about the gender gap, being able to be explicit about it and actually having research that proved its existence made a very big difference. 'It was a good opportunity,' said Gibson. 'We did have these Labour Party statistics, not anybody else's, but the Labour Party itself, saying we haven't got enough of the women's vote . . . that obviously helped us.' Rooney agreed. 'I think it was convenient in the sense that it helped people at the top of the Labour Party actually to be convinced.' She leaned back in her chair and smiled. 'I have been around long enough that I don't care why somebody does something, as long as it's the right thing to do.'

The six trades union women who sat together on the NEC women's committee believed unanimously that putting women into positions of power would deliver a better deal for women as a whole in the country. As paid representatives, however, they had to be careful to reflect the views of their unions in their public statements. And in spite of two manu-facturing recessions, a shift to flexible, part-time work, and the general 'feminisation' of the marketplace, women were still only a minority within the movement.

Angela Eagle's union, the Confederation of Health Service Employees (COHSE), and NUPE, where O'Mara worked, were exceptional, with women representing 79 per cent and 75 per cent of total membership respectively. But in MSF the proportion dropped to 19 per cent. Prosser and Rooney's unions, the TGWU and the AEEU, lagged even further be-hind. Before they could argue for quotas at Party conference, Rooney, Prosser, O'Mara, Gibson, Eagle and Bernadette Hillon at the Union of Shop, Distributive and Allied Workers (USDAW) had to get the policy supported by their own organisations.

Gibson's union, MSF, had always been in favour of the idea, but over at the Engineering Union Rooney had her work cut out. 'Leadership sometimes means that you can help people formulate policy,' she told me, 'you can plant an idea with a woman in a factory somewhere and say, "Do you think that this is an idea that we should be looking at as a union?"' You can have ideas, she said, and feed them through the sausage machine and eventually they become the policy of the union. 'And this is what we did in the Engineering Union the year we actually got support for all-women shortlists, which was no mean task.'

They met informally in the Piano Bar of the Marlborough Hotel every six weeks or so, and plotted and planned, work-ing out, as Prosser said proudly, 'how we were going to sup-port each other, just the same as men have done, over the years'. The meetings were an opportunity for them to sound off their frustrations, but also, more importantly, to exchange ideas. 'We would think – this is a good idea, let's test it,' said Gibson. 'Or I would say, "I would find that very difficult, but I'll take it back and see what our women's committee say." And then we'd come back again and compare notes as to how we were doing. So, yes, it was a two-way process. Because if we didn't take our women with us in our unions we wouldn't have got anywhere at the [Party] conference.'

The policy had to be tracked through every union's annual conference. Some members were caught on the hop, particularly in the Engineers' Union where, according to Rooney, people gave support to it grudgingly. Members found they had to say the right thing to get a platform for themselves and ended up voting in favour of a policy whose full implications they didn't really understand; the same thing happened at Labour Party conferences too. O'Mara remembers getting up in a fringe meeting held after the 1990 Party conference had decided in favour of the NEC's proposals on quotas and asking, 'Has anybody read this Composite? Do you realise what we've agreed to here today?' I asked her what their reaction was. 'People just laughed, just laughed.'

In fact the policy they had voted for would bring radical change. The details had yet to be worked out, but in principle, from now on, 40 per cent of positions, at every level of the Party, from NEC to CLP, had to go to women. A few Party members simply didn't believe it would happen, O'Mara told me. They complained when the rule-book came back changed. 'And of course you said to them, "Well if you didn't like it, why did you vote for it?"' It was very painful, particularly at the CLP level. 'People would get up and say – "Bloody quotas, we haven't got any women who want to be in these positions. And we've got Bill here, he wants to do it, and you're saying he can't do it because it's got to be a woman?" So at that level, it was unpleasant, it was painful.'

Prosser stood firm when people complained to her about the scandal of having to keep seats vacant because they couldn't find women to fill them. 'What have you done to encourage women to come forward? What education programmes have you put on? What have you done about ensuring that

148

women have got transport to get to meetings?' she used to reply.

'Oh, where are we going to find all these women from?' became the annual cry. But they have found them. 'They do a good job and their unions are perfectly happy,' O'Mara said. In the unions, and in the Labour Party too. 'Now you look down at Party conference: 50 per cent of the delegates are women. You look at the platform: 50 per cent are women. And the good thing about it is, I always said, when that happened, for once women would stop standing out simply because they were women. They would start standing out on the basis of their ability.'

By the late 1980s, then, it was clear that quotas for women was an idea whose time had come. Behind the scenes, the trades union women had worked successfully to bring their organisations round to support it. Party officers like Joyce Gould and Peter Coleman (successive Directors of Organisation) and Larry Whitty (General Secretary), who could have blocked the policy, proved sympathetic instead. A series of dynamic National Women's Officers, Vicky Phillips, Val Shawcross, and Deborah Lincoln, also supported it strongly.

Moreover, the policy had been finding favour with Party leadership, and not just because of the electoral advantages to be gained by closing the gender gap. After the 1987 election Neil Kinnock appointed more than half of the Labour women MPs to his front bench. O'Mara did not know what Mr Kinnock's views on quotas were, 'All I know is that we were never told that we couldn't do these things.' After Kinnock stood down, John Smith was also, crucially, supportive. 'He had a very direct approach – that if it was right you had to do it, even though it was going to be really difficult,' said Hilary Armstrong, his Parliamentary Private Secretary. 'He wasn't happy, in that he never liked doing things that the Party was going to find difficult, but he was determined.'

In 1989 conference voted overwhelmingly in support of Composite 54, but the priority in terms of making the Labour Party more appealing to women voters was still to increase the number, and heighten the profile, of women MPs. The question now was how, positively, to go about getting them.

Two Fabian pamphlets, published in consecutive years, set out the alternatives. In *Women's Votes: The Key to Winning*, Patricia Hewitt and Deborah Mattinson argued that the right of constituency parties to choose their own candidate was overriding. The Party, they said, should respect this right and avoid compulsion, particularly since 'positive discrimination in candidate selection would almost certainly be unlawful under the Sex Discrimination Act'. Instead Labour should 'follow the example of its European sister parties and adopt a target of 40 per cent women MPs by the end of the century. Although the target would not, and could not, force any individual constituency party to select a woman in preference to a man, it would help to concentrate the minds of Labour Party members on the need to select more women candidates, particularly in safe and winnable seats.'

Rachel Brooks, Angela Eagle and Clare Short had different ideas. In *Quotas Now: Women in the Labour Party*, they argued that simply persuading women to get involved in politics had already failed. Although well aware that 'no plan of affirmative action works well if it is resented and resisted', they went on to say that 'quotas must be enforced if they are to be effective'. The pamphlet concluded with a list of fourteen recommendations, advocating the continued application of quotas to all levels of the Party, changes to the rules for selecting candidates, and the speedy adoption of a policy of all-women shortlists in 'some' parliamentary seats.

The turning point came in 1992 when Labour lost the election. Kinnock stepped down, to be replaced by Smith and promises of reform. Labour's thirty-seven women MPs started meeting regularly to discuss a variety of 'women's issues', including the problem of representation, and a subcommittee of the NEC Women's Committee finally hit on a compromise on the question of all-women shortlists.

According to O'Mara, it was Short who came up with the solution: regional targets, where half the safe seats and half the winnable seats in every region would be committed to an

all-women shortlist. 'This was the only way to be fair to popular male candidates who had fought previously, protect local
choice and secure a guaranteed advance in women's representation,' remembers Short. Dividing the country into regions,
they hoped enough constituencies would volunteer for all-
women shortlists to make compulsion unnecessary. 'It wasn't
very radical,' O'Mara mused, but there were always going to
be problems.

The first problem was getting conference to agree. 'The
Labour Party will today enter a labyrinth of complex rule
changes and composite motions in an effort to resolve
OMOV, the leadership's attempt to change the party into a
"one member, one vote" democracy,' Patrick Wintour
announced to readers of the *Guardian* in late September
1993. It was a reform John Smith had publicly staked his
leadership on, and pundits believed the vote might very easily
go either way.

Among members of the NEC Women's Committee and the
Parliamentary Labour Party (PLP) women's group, tensions
also ran high. The policy had been tracked and endorsed all
the way up through the ranks to the NEC. With the unions
holding the lion's share of the conference vote and the leadership on board, it seemed a sure thing. Then Larry Whitty's
proposed running order for the conference came through. The
changes in the constitution, on OMOV and all-women shortlists, had been joined together in one debate.

Reactions to this development varied. Rooney couldn't
believe her luck. The AEEU had been campaigning for
OMOV for a long time, but it didn't support all-women
shortlists. Now it was a case of voting for neither or both. 'It
was just accepted that we would vote for both.' But Gibson,
over at MSF, was horrified. 'It was all in the booklet', she told
me, 'muddled up. It wasn't just one section saying this means
that women can do X, Y and Z. There was a bit here, a bit
there, a bit there.' The position in MSF was black to the
AEEU's white, and Gibson could see the anti-OMOV lobby
winning the day. Suddenly it looked like all their work was
going be wiped out by nothing more than a piece of clumsy

drafting.

Hilary Armstrong remembers the proposal coming through to John Smith's office. 'We had an emergency meeting immediately,' she said. 'We thought this was a conspiracy to see it go down, or that it could be used by conspirators.' Did she think OMOV and all-women shortlists had been put together deliberately? No, 'We went back and talked to Larry,' she said, 'and Larry said, "No, this is the way we always do it, the way you change the constitution is this, this, and this."'

Lincoln agreed. The drafting wasn't clumsy, it was meticulous. The debate on all-women shortlists was bound up with OMOV because 'that was where it should have been, that was how it fitted together and when the thing was being written initially, it wasn't about working the votes out, it was about how should it all be pieced together, how should it work together'.

Meticulous and, in Gibson's words, 'very clever of the Party'. 'Oh, there was no accident about the drafting,' she said. The political imperative for them was to get the one member, one vote stuff through. So they linked it with all-women shortlists deliberately as a way to get more union votes? 'Oh yeah, oh yeah', said Prosser. 'A lot of people saw it as a political fix.' For a Party in the midst of a series of very public, supposedly democratic reforms, it did not look good, and as the union blocks lined up, it became clear that the vote was going to be very close.

It is usually only when the sides are evenly matched that individuals get to change the course of history. In 1993 Anne Gibson turned out to be this pivotal person. Her union, MSF, was still undecided. 'If we voted against, then we voted all the women's proposals down. And if we voted in favour, then we directly voted against our conference policy on one member, one vote. Right up to the very end we were arguing,' she said, 'and then we got to know, on the morning of the day the vote was going to be taken, that it looked as if our vote would be the crucial one.'

O'Mara, meanwhile, was working on a safety net. At the last minute, someone had spotted Resolution 417, a six-liner moved by John Fletcher on behalf of Coventry South-West, which also supported all-women shortlists. Knowing full well what might happen to OMOV, she got NUPE to second it. If they lost OMOV, she said, they 'would then go to the NEC later in the afternoon and say, "Look, there is this resolution that was carried earlier in the day." It's a little obscure', she admits, and she wasn't sure whether the NEC would take any notice, but at least it meant they would have a second bite at the cherry.

The MSF delegation was bombarded with faxes. On 29 September they called an urgent officers' meeting, in which Gibson made her position very clear. 'I said I was quite ready to stick my neck out. I didn't like doing it, but I would go against the OMOV conference policy if necessary because I felt so strongly, and I believed the majority of MSF women would feel as strongly, about the women's area.' She spoke again at a further delegation meeting, held at lunchtime, and finally after eighty minutes they voted by nineteen to seventeen to abstain.

'As we were leaving the room, someone said, "Shouldn't somebody go to the rest and explain why a big union like us is abstaining?" And the General Secretary said, "You know the answers Anne, you go."' The atmosphere in the conference hall was tense. 'When we got back in they were waiting,' she said. 'I mean obviously waiting. And I just put up my hand, as I walked in the door, to speak'. Friends from the General Municipal and Boilermakers (GMB) called out to her, 'Oh no, Anne, it's not going to be you is it?' as she walked up to the platform. 'Watch this space,' she answered. She remembers 'waving the paper and saying, "Women should not be used as pawns in men's games," and there was a great roar went up from the floor and a lot of the women started stamping and whistling and shouting and things. Because we were used as that, there's no doubt about it.

'I suppose I did know how important it was in one sense, but I was so tied up with wanting to get through for women generally, I didn't realise how big a political thing, with a capital P, it would become.' Not until afterwards. 'And then I remember Mo Mowlam coming down and putting her arm round my shoulders and saying, "You're going to have a tough time, mate, for the next few months. If you want any help, you know, just give me a call." And I said, "Oh, it will be all right, Mo," very nonchalantly. And then I saw the papers the next day.'

She chuckled thinking of the headlines. 'The story went that Hilary Armstrong had rung her old mate Anne Gibson and said something to the words "Save John's life", because he had said he was going to resign if he lost the vote. And so I went along and persuaded my delegation. And it was my vote. Which was silly, because I didn't vote, you know. We abstained!'

Whoever she did it for, everyone agrees that Gibson played a crucial role. Conference wound up on the Friday and John Smith called her in to thank her in person for what she had done. He said, 'You won't only go down in the history of the Labour movement, you'll go down in the history of John Smith.' But Mowlam was right. 'At my union conference the next year, the delegation were castigated for voting the way they did,' said Gibson. 'Me in particular.' She was berated at MSF annual conferences for three years running. 'But there we are. That's life.'

9

THE QUOTA-WOMEN

SEPTEMBER 29TH, 1993 WAS an emotional day, but what did people think of the policy afterwards, when the press moved on and temperatures had cooled?

'By and large it was well received,' said Gibson. 'The funny thing is, of course, it was well received because lots of men, even bright, intelligent, clued-up men in the House of Commons, for example, didn't realise what it meant. They hadn't been following the debate.' The morning after the momentous OMOV vote, she had breakfast with one of the union's MPs, a man who shall remain nameless. Conference was still very much on their minds, the obvious subject of conversation. 'That that went through yesterday, I've been reading it – I don't think much of it,' the MP told her. Which part, she wondered? 'Oh, the women's. It means there's going to be some constituencies where you can't get a man on the short-list, doesn't it?'

'Well, yeah, that's what all this has been about,' answered Gibson patiently.

'That's disgraceful. That is quite wrong. I mean, I couldn't have supported that,' he said.

This is the sort of story Deborah Lincoln hates to hear. 'There are always people who'll play the odds,' she shrugged. And there were always going to be one or two people who didn't understand what they were voting for. She insists that no one was deliberately misled. 'At that conference one of my roles was to ensure that everyone was absolutely clear and that we went for the high ground, we went for the arguments.

Clare certainly felt very strongly that if people didn't know what they'd voted for then in the end it would unravel.' Although they had to work hard to make sure it went through, she believes they won through the arguments, because 'in the end this is too big an issue to be fixed'.

Even so, the *Guardian* reported 'angry exchanges', quoting John Spellar MP: 'Where will it end? With ethnic quotas? It won't help one bit to win the next election.' According to O'Mara, the policy was 'not without controversy, and a lot of people were very angry and hurt about it. A lot of men were very worried, who felt that they were going to have their one and only chance taken away from them.'

Just how 'angry and hurt', Lincoln herself discovered in the months that followed. In 1993 conference committed the Party to a radical set of selection-process reforms. In 1994 it approved a procedure for their implementation. It had been Lincoln's idea to hold regional consensus meetings to decide which seats should have all-women shortlists and now, with constituencies keen to make their candidate selections as soon as possible, the pressure was on to go out and 'sell' the policy. She and Peter Coleman went round each of the regions, speaking to representatives. It was a painstaking, delicate task. 'We began with a presentation, presenting the reasoning behind it, the history, the whys and the wherefores and what we wanted them to do and agree, and then we just talked to them – tried basically to get people to volunteer.'

Of the thirty-five women MPs actually elected from all-women shortlists, twenty said their constituencies had volunteered for them, for a variety of reasons. In some, the local Party already knew they wanted a woman. According to Kali Mountford, the Colne Valley CLP was aware of who the other candidates would be, and applied for an all-women shortlist because they 'wanted to present the Labour Party as fresh and different'. 'It fitted their plans,' she said.

Diana Organ had stood in the Forest of Dean in 1992, and the CLP there wanted her to try again; so when the question of shortlists came up, they were more than happy to volunteer. Plymouth, Sutton, Nancy Astor's old constituency, 'certainly was the first seat in the country to go very willingly for an all-women shortlist', Linda Gilroy told me. 'At the meeting which was called I think only one person voted against it.'

Other CLPs volunteered quickly because they feared there would only be a limited supply of quality candidates. Judy Mallaber told me that in her seat, Amber Valley, a marginal, the CLP had actually voted against the policy at the Party conference. In 1994 they decided to opt for an all-women shortlist after all, because 'they would probably end up having to do it later on, so they might as well go in early, when there was a chance of getting people'. An unfounded anxiety, as it turned out. According to Gisela Stuart 'something like over fifty women' applied with her for Birmingham Edgbaston, one of the very first to volunteer. But there were other reasons to act fast. Although the Labour folk in Northampton North politely never raised shortlists 'as an issue' to Sally Keeble's face, she suspects 'the constituency had basically done it for pragmatic reasons, because they wanted to get their candidates selected early so they could get on with campaigning'.

'A lot of the yeses and nos, frankly, were about whether there was a favoured woman or a favoured man,' said Lincoln. In Beverley Hughes's constituency, Stretford and Urmston, the CLP 'had voted very narrowly as a matter of principle not to be a women only shortlist' and there were two local men who, it was felt, had the right to stand. Unable to find sufficient volunteers, the region's officers decided that an all-women shortlist must be imposed. 'I felt very uncomfortable,' Hughes told me. Although she supported the policy and sympathised completely with the reasoning behind it, she still hates the thought of people saying she had a leg-up. 'Inside me I smart at the idea that somebody could say that.'

Falmouth and Camborne went for an all-women shortlist early on and selected Candy Atherton, but there was one man in particular who believed that the seat was his. John Geach fought a running battle effectively right through, up to and including election day. Lincoln remembers it well. There was a real furore and it was up to her to go down and talk to the CLP.

Bob Cryer's old constituency, Keighley, suffered similar disruption. The Party officers opted for the policy without consulting their general committee. When it was finally informed all hell was let loose. 'I mean talk about the night of the long knives and blood on the floor,' remembers Cryer's widow, Ann. Eventually, after much persuasion, she put her name forward for the seat as the compromise candidate. 'Some of the people who nominated me had been the opponents of the all-women shortlist,' she said. 'They felt I satisfied both sides. It was oil on troubled waters.'

Of the CLPs which volunteered, Lincoln concluded, 'What we ended up with was, at least in part, the ones that you might have expected.' A lot of the local parties felt it was their duty to support the policy because conference had already agreed it. When the delegates and Chairs from the regional groups went off into huddles to decide between them who was going to volunteer, they nearly always came back with an answer, she told me. She was proud of the overall response. Even so, it was 'very, very difficult for some people to accept because, essentially, what it's saying is that the Party wasn't capable, and individuals weren't capable, of making a choice that wasn't based on gender', she said. People do not like to be told there is discrimination within their Party. They think they have always selected candidates on the basis of ability. 'But then,' said Lincoln, 'since men were five times more likely to be selected, does that suggest that women are five times more stupid?'

Male candidates started to write in, saying, 'My future has been destroyed by you.' Ann Carlton and Nicola Kutapan set up Labour Supporters for Real Equality (LSRE), and launched their campaign against all-women shortlists in the press. As Lincoln admits, 'It was always much more easy for people to be critical.' 'The PR campaign that they actually waged was pretty effective,' she said, 'you know, [the suggestion that] that you are essentially excluding men.' Carlton, naturally, agreed. 'Gradually we found we were winning the argument.'

'I think we lost some ground there,' said Lincoln. 'Because

it was the right thing to do, because the NEC were in favour of it, because the Party had agreed to it, because conference had said so, there wasn't the same impetus for us as for those who were against it to go out and talk about it in the press.' And, precisely for those very same reasons, the press was the only place left where LSRE could make their case. If it was debate within the Party they wanted, they had missed the boat.

Perhaps this explains why the newspaper headlines descended into bitterness and ferocity as the campaign progressed. From LABOUR WOMEN WANT EQUALITY – NOT SPECIAL TREATMENT, to LABOUR'S ALL-WOMEN POLICY 'A VOTE LOSER'.

Married to Llanelli MP Denzil Davies and herself a former political adviser to Tony Crosland and John Silkin, Carlton was a newspaper editor's dream. Opponent, insider, feminist (I asked her). 'In an astonishing attack on members of her own Party, a senior Labour figure argues that women-only quotas could lose Tony Blair the next general election,' boasted the sub to an article in the *Daily Mail* headed up WHY I DESPISE THESE SELFISH WIMMIN.

On her side, Carlton complained about 'the sheer personal unpleasantness' some Party members encountered. 'The men who stood up and said, "We don't approve," were told that they were sexist. The women who spoke up were also browbeaten. There were all sorts of abusive things said to individuals. We became a focal point of considerable abuse by setting up this organisation,' she told me. 'But it did give other people the courage to go ahead and say things.'

Lincoln acknowledges that it was a hard policy and there were plenty of times when things looked scary. But in the end, she believes, they had actually won people over. Angela Eagle was amazed it was so easy. 'There was actually far less trouble about it than I had expected,' she told me. 'We did it from scratch in three years, which is extraordinarily fast.' Conference voted overwhelmingly in favour of the policy in 1994 and afterwards the NEC issued a statement reaffirming its view 'that if the Labour Party is truly to reflect the communities it seeks to represent there must be a significant improvement in the level of women's representation in parliament'.

In the week of 3 February 1995, the newly created constituency of Regent's Park and Kensington North placed an advertisement for prospective parliamentary candidates in *Tribune* magazine. Part-time law lecturer Peter Jepson applied and was rejected because the CLP were only nominating women. One month later an industrial tribunal gave him leave to challenge the decision under the 1975 Sex Discrimination Act and the 1976 European Union directive on equal treatment. Naturally the Party had taken legal advice before the policy was even written up. It had proceeded on the grounds that political parties are, in effect, exempt from the requirements of the Act, although officials knew very well that they could never be absolutely certain until it was tested. 'There wasn't any precedent,' said Lincoln. 'This had never been done before.' 'We expect the challenge to be defeated, but the action is yet to be heard,' Short wrote at the time.

BLOOD ON CARPET AS THE SISTERS ADVANCE ran the headline to a *Guardian* article published on April Fools' Day that year, announcing the selection of eleven women candidates under the new procedure. 'Elsewhere Walworth Road boasts that 40 per cent of those constituencies where the issue has been addressed have signed up for the quota system.' It was hard work, with some constituencies in the north-west region threatening to unite in opposition to the policy, but overall things seemed to be going well. Then came Slough.

As Lincoln and Coleman were learning, attitudes to all-women shortlists very much depended on whether the local CLP had unofficially selected its candidate already and, if so, upon that person's sex. In Slough the unofficial candidate was Eddie Lopez, a political agent and well-known left-winger who had fought the seat in the previous two elections and, in the eyes of many, been cheated of victory in 1992 when former councillor, Declan Alford, put himself forward as an Independent Labour candidate and scraped up 699 votes.

John Watts, Conservative, won the seat with a majority of 514. Now, in 1995, it was considered highly winnable.

According to Slough Party Chairman, Mike Thorpe, the CLP had 'nothing against women'. Even so, the General Committee 'voted by 70 to 4 to reject an all-women's list' and female Party members declared themselves particularly hostile to the policy. Opposition consolidated and dug in. This was exactly what Lincoln and Coleman had been hoping to avoid. On 24 May the NEC held firm to the policy and ordered them to impose an all-women shortlist on the Berkshire constituency. An example was to be made of them.

Meanwhile opposition in the north-west region rumbled on. So far only one of the twelve target seats had volunteered, and local Party members were muttering that disappointed male candidates might split the Labour vote by running as independents. Tony Blair's July announcement that the policy would be abandoned after the next general election may have been intended to encourage co-operation in the region; instead, it had the opposite effect. The rebellious CLPs smelled blood. Slough had finally made its nominations from an all-women list in August, but people were predicting the selection would go to Eddie Lopez's wife, Brenda, the protest candidate. 'Local Party members have described the policy as dictatorial, discriminatory, racist and undemocratic, and I agree with them,' she told reporters. A European Court of Justice ruling that quotas advancing the promotion of women were in breach of European Law encouraged Jepson and his supporters to press ahead with their case.

When it came, Lincoln remembers being almost surprised by the instruction to appear before an Industrial Tribunal in Leeds in the third week of December. The Party had always thought there was a very strong likelihood that the policy would be tried at law, but 'as it didn't happen and didn't happen I think it's fair to say we began to believe it wasn't going to be tested', she said.

Though championed by a number of constituency parties, Jepson brought the case himself, as an individual. A canny move, as things turned out. He wasn't a QC, but he wasn't the ignorant layman he appeared to be either. In fact he was working on a PhD in discrimination law and lectured part-time at University College London. He managed his case adroitly and became the focus of considerable attention. 'I think one of the factors that definitely came into play was the fact that we had very senior counsel, and he was like the Lone Ranger.' As the Chair of the Tribunal seemed to see it, it was a case of the machine versus the individual, and the individual won.

At the start of the hearing the Party had said that, in the unlikely event of it losing the case, it would appeal. Immediately after the ruling, however, exactly what should happen next was far from clear. Lincoln went down to read out their statement to the press. 'It was a pretty horrendous moment,' she remembers. Counsel advised that an appeal could still go either way and would further disrupt the selection process in as many as seventy constituencies. With a general election looming in 1997, at the very latest, no one wanted that. Secure in their knowledge that the position of the thirty-eight new women candidates already selected from the shortlists would remain unaffected by the Tribunal's decision, the NEC voted unanimously not to appeal. 'I think we all felt that the right thing to do was to stop, because we'd achieved what needed to be achieved,' said Lincoln. Angela Eagle agreed. 'I understood why we didn't appeal, but I still think the ruling was a complete nonsense and I think, had it been challenged, it would have been shown to be.' The candidates needed to get on with doing their jobs, and to keep going on and on and on about selection was just not helpful.

The NEC issued a statement comparing the 132 women, sitting and new, selected so far by Labour with the Conservatives' five candidates. 'It is in stark contrast with the abysmal record of the Tory Party and is something of which we can be rightly proud.'

On 31 January 1996 the NEC agreed unanimously not to appeal against the Leeds Industrial Tribunal ruling. The policy was scrapped. Ten constituencies had to start choosing their candidates all over again. Lorna Fitzsimons, in

Rochdale, was lucky. There the selection process had only just got started when the decision came through, and the constituency hadn't really wanted an all-women shortlist anyway. 'The only reason they chose it was to stop them getting the candidate that they had had for the past two general elections, which was a man.' Even so, the CLP's reaction to the change of policy was odd. 'All of a sudden it was as if they themselves had chosen and designed all-women shortlists and who was the national Party to tell them they couldn't have a woman? It was quite funny,' she remembers.

For others, the switch was altogether more difficult. When the City of Chester CLP advertised for a woman candidate, Christine Russell was the only constituency woman to apply. In spite of an influential but disappointed male constituency member canvassing for one of her opponents, she won it easily with a majority of 84 per cent and set about recruiting her campaign team. She'd been a candidate for six or so weeks when the bombshell dropped. There had been a cock-up at Walworth Road and someone had forgotten to forward her selection papers to the December GMC for ratification. Now that all-women shortlists had been declared in breach of the law, the whole selection would have to be re-opened. And the second time round, of course, she'd have to fight her male rival directly since nothing, not even a call from John Prescott, could persuade him not to stand. In the end she won again, with the same majority, but four months of important constituency groundwork had been lost.

In Joan Humble's Blackpool North and Fleetwood constituency the final selection meeting had been scheduled to take place the week after the tribunal decision. But in spite of having to go through virtually the whole process twice, she told me, she was glad to have been selected on an open shortlist in the end. Geraldine Smith, who took Morecambe and Lunesdale from the Conservatives with a 6,000 majority, expressed a similar ambivalence. The policy was a necessity, she said, but she was pleased her own selection was from a mixed list 'because no one could use that against me in the general election'. Jane Griffiths told me she was quite keen that her constituency, Reading East, shouldn't have an all-women shortlist, 'because I thought if we did, people would say – oh well, you only got it because you're a woman'.

This was the Conservatives' line of argument too. According to Eleanor Laing, the policy was equivalent to saying 'men can swim on their own but women always need to be wearing water wings'. Of the thirty-five shortlist MPs she told me: 'Their male colleagues will say – oh yes, so and so, well you know, she's OK for sitting on the backbenches but she wouldn't have got here if it hadn't been for the all-women shortlists – and so you're always a second-class Member.'

Ann Widdecombe agreed. 'I certainly haven't sat down and worked out who it is who came in on an all-women shortlist, but the fact is that there are some women on that side of the House who have got there on exactly the same basis as the men and there are some who have not. And in time we may see that starting to make a difference. That may start to be used as a taunt.'

It may, but so far Members of Parliament on both sides of the House have been overwhelmingly supportive of the new women MPs. And as for being second-class citizens, Judy Mallaber told me, 'Nobody has even raised the question.' Many of those who had tried for candidacies through both selection processes told me the standard of competition was actually higher on the all-women lists. As Phyllis Starkey says, 'The interesting thing about the all-women shortlist was that gender was then not an issue, whereas if you're standing as a woman in an open shortlist you can make a point of how important it is to have more women MPs. Obviously, with an all-women shortlist that is entirely irrelevant, and the selection is just on the abilities of the individual woman.'

Jean Corston elaborated. With shortlists of four or five women, 'constituency parties discovered they weren't just being offered the choice of a woman candidate, one of five. They were actually being offered a choice of very different politicians who happened to be women and finally, I think, it broke through this notion that women are just one particular type of politician.'

Charlotte Atkins told me she certainly did not think a women-only shortlist was an easy option. 'In fact, a lot of people were advising me that probably I'd find it easier in the mixed shortlist,' she said.

Though almost all of Labour's 101 women MPs said they had supported the policy, far fewer expressed unqualified approval. And fewer still agreed with Linda Perham, who 'could see it was the only way we were going to get more women in parliament and I haven't got any sympathy with the men, I'm afraid. Parliament's been peopled with mediocre men for centuries. And, you know, the worry about, "We might get women who aren't quite up to it . . .", too bad. There's lots of men who aren't up to it. Nobody gives up power willingly, you know.'

Ann Taylor's view was more commonly held. 'I think we were all supporters, it's a question of how enthusiastic,' she told me. 'I wasn't particularly enthusiastic, and went along with them as a device on a temporary basis.' Bridget Prentice and Anne Campbell felt the same. 'I don't think any of us actually wanted to do it,' said Margaret Beckett. 'It's just that we weren't making enough progress.' A lot of the women MPs I spoke to agreed with Jean Corston that 'it was a very necessary process'. 'I think most of us were not terribly gung-ho about it,' said Hazel Blears, 'but the things that militate against women being chosen are so deep-rooted that you had to kick-start it'.

According to Cheryl Gillan, Conservative MP for Chesham and Amersham, more and more women were finding their way to parliament anyway, without any kind of intervention from above. 'It's always been a slow process, but the progress for women has always been in the right direction.' But who has time to wait? Not Claire Curtis-Thomas. 'I feel very angry that I will have been dead for so long before women of ability get to a position where they can exercise that ability. The all-women shortlist at least allowed us to leapfrog a century.'

It has also changed the political climate within the Labour Party for good, as Angela Eagle pointed out. Through the actual process of debating the arguments in favour of positive

165

discrimination: 'You persuade most reasonable people that something's got to be done.' And even after the policy was outlawed, 'We still got women elected and we had voluntary women-only shortlists and more women came through anyway. I think we've made an enormous cultural change and I think it's going to be very difficult indeed for that to be rolled back, and I might add that I don't think that there are many men left in the Labour Party who would want to roll it back.'

For such a short-lived policy, it is likely that all-women shortlists will have disproportionately far-reaching effects, both inside and outside the House. So far-reaching, in fact, that almost everyone I spoke to agreed that there would be no need to try and revive it. All-women shortlists were 'just a short-term thing', an 'extra boost'. 120 out of 659, it seems, is a critical mass. Our women MPs can take it on from here alone.

'I think we look more than our size proportionately, because people are so surprised at seeing us,' said Judy Mallaber. 'It would be very easy for people to get complacent.' According to Shona McIsaac, 'what we've got to do now is to be role models for women coming up through the Party. Even within Cleethorpes Labour Party, and with the wee girls in the area, I've seen a change in their attitude already.' The girls, she says, eight to twelve year olds, 'think it's cool. They keep coming round saying, "It's cool . . . we got a girl, we got a woman!" And they think this is great.'

So does Deborah Lincoln. I had wondered whether she felt at all bitter or betrayed that the policy had been dropped so quickly. 'No,' she said, suddenly pragmatic. In a way, the story of all-women shortlists is a kind of political parable with brothers and sisters fighting each other in the name of justice, and a happy ending after all. 'I felt a sense of huge celebration. I feel very proud of my Party. I think we've done an amazing job. It was all I thought about for years – but actually it worked. I felt proud.'

10

A NEW BROOM

THE PALACE OF Westminster is a deeply traditional place. Along with Buckingham Palace and Madam Tussaud's, it is an important stop on the London tourist route. It is also the hard-working heart of British government. The streets around it are jammed with people from every country in the world, armed with cameras and guide-books, eager to look at, to snap, and if possible visit the Commons and the Lords, to experience the Mother of Parliaments for themselves.

Every day, before the House of Commons reassembles, a respectfully bemused, delighted crowd gathers in Central Lobby to watch the Speaker's Procession. MPs and their constituents down on official business are commanded to stand motionless, along with the rest. The policemen take their helmets off, and out of a buzzing silence comes the sharp, brisk click of heels in synch. Betty Boothroyd, only child of Yorkshire millworkers, former Tiller girl, House of Commons Secretary, MP for West Bromwich West since 1974, and first woman Speaker of the House, is making her entrance.

'I never felt I was going to become Speaker, I have to tell you very honestly about that. I was asked a very long time ago by Speaker Wetherall if I would become Chairman of Speaker's panel chairing standing committees – the legislation that is going through the House upstairs – and I said, yes I'd like to do that, so I did it for a very long time. And then there was a vacancy as Deputy Speaker in, I think it was 1987, and I was invited to become Deputy Speaker and that was of course very thrilling and even then I never felt I would become Speaker of this House. In fact I didn't really feel it until 1992, when we came back and a lot of my colleagues said you ought to run, you know, you ought to have a go. And I've always done things by faith and daring and I had faith in myself, and I thought let me dare the Commons to see what they're going to do.'

Former Cabinet Minister Peter Brooke was the Conservative's official candidate to replace Speaker Wetherall, but the Party was divided. Proposed by John Biffen and seconded by her old friend Gwyneth Dunwoody, Betty Boothroyd won by 134 votes.

In the first few weeks of the 1997 Labour government chaos reigned. New Members could be seen perched on window-ledges, propped against walls and hiding behind sofas. They were instantly recognisable. They all carried bursting bundles of post and phones tucked under chins. Complaints about the accommodation were legion, compliments hard to find.

According to Maria Eagle, the point when you have just been elected – when there is maximum interest in what you are doing, and people want you to help them – is exactly the point where it becomes almost impossible for a new MP to respond to requests. You cannot give people a phone number to call you back. You cannot write letters very easily. For the first few weeks Eagle wrote all of hers by hand.

Caroline Flint, on her first-ever report back to her constituency Labour Party a month after she was elected, announced triumphantly that she had been given a window-less room seven feet by ten, and that she and her partner Phil had been out to buy a computer and printer.

Many of the new women came from powerful positions in local government, business and the trade unions. They found Westminster cumbersome and old-fashioned and hard to get to grips with. In the first month there were many anguished calls for instant reform. Away from the public eye, the Serjeant-at-Arms and his staff, who are responsible for accommodation and the smooth running of the Palace, worked desperately to give everyone an office and a phone. They had been on the go twenty-four hours a day, since seven-thirty on the morning of 2 May, when the occupants of 10 Downing Street phoned in and asked how soon they could be moved out.

Jill Pay, the Head Office Keeper, said it wasn't as simple as handing out a few packing cases. The Labour landslide had been so huge that many Members who had been at Westminster for decades found themselves moving out unexpectedly, and hundreds of their staff were made unemployed overnight. Many needed a sympathetic ear along with the packing cases. Others felt so humiliated by their fate that they asked to come in and pack up at strange hours, so they could avoid their colleagues.

New Labour Members are the first generation of 'on-message' MPs. Each has been issued with a pager stamped with the party logo, a red rose and the word Labour. Clipped on the waistband of skirt or trousers, it's a very visible symbol of change. Austin Mitchell MP, desperate rebel that he is, still hasn't picked up his pager from the Labour Party resource centre. Presumably it lies forgotten in some drawer accumulating thousands of instructions to vote. Or not to vote. To come to the Prime Minister's office immediately. To stay away. To nip over to Number 11 with some advice for Gordon Brown. However exciting it is, New Labour's message to him lies ignored.

'Mother' of the House, Gwyneth Dunwoody is sympathetic. At sixty-eight, with twenty-seven years' service to her name, she is the Commons' most senior woman MP. 'I don't regard gadgets, the carrying of a pager or the bleeping of the telephone as a demonstration of any particular intelligence or any ability to do things efficiently. I regard it as (a sign of) someone who loves having toys. I was a bit stunned by the acquiescent way in which the new Members trotted in and got their bleepers from the Whips' Office.'

She pointed to another New Labour change. 'We got a letter today which is hilarious. Tells me when I may take a week off, and it picks Budget week, presumably because they don't want me to discuss the Budget. Well, frankly that is a misunderstanding of the way MPs operate . . .'

Mrs Dunwoody's letter was from the Chief Whip, Nick Brown. Because Labour has a huge majority and new Members were complaining loudly about late night votes and long hours at Westminster, he hit on the idea of giving Members a week off each term to work in their constituencies. For new Members with empty engagement diaries, this was fine. A chance to catch up. For old hands like Gwyneth and Austin, this was a nonsense. It took no account at all of engagements in London made months or years before. But no one was listening much to old Members, male or female.

As May turned to June and new Members got some sleep and discovered the delights of strawberries and cream and Pimms on the Terrace overlooking the Thames, life became calmer. Complaints about phones and offices dwindled and began to be replaced with serious calls for reform at Westminster.

The government announced that the Leader of the House, Ann Taylor, would head a modernisation committee, which would report quickly. This won general approval. New Member Phyllis Starkey has been appointed to the committee: 'Parliament is about getting government legislation through but allowing the opposition a proper opportunity to voice their opposition, and allowing all MPs to have an input into the legislation to make sure it works properly, and I think it's important that we keep that upfront. The way in which the business is done in the House should be made as clear and efficient as possible and that means being much more flexible about the way legislation is dealt with.'

Starkey told us, and the committee soon announced, that the Order Paper, the daily running order or timetable of Commons life was going to be made more readable. 'If an ordinary new Member picked it up, she would be able to understand it.' This had to be good news. The long hours and the lack of timetabling were cited by many women as the biggest problems of being a Westminster MP.

Joan Walley is an enthusiast for reform. She moved her

family from London to her constituency in Stoke-on-Trent when she was elected ten years ago. Every Monday she leaves her husband and teenage sons and goes off to Westminster. She is, she says, 'really fed up' with the assumption that by 'modernising', people envisage some 'kind of nine to five working week based in parliament'. According to Walley, 'This is completely the wrong way of doing it and it doesn't tie in with other experiences in parliaments elsewhere.' She would like parliament to sit mid-week only, so that MPs can spend two full weekdays in their constituencies. 'We want MPs who are in touch with their constituents and have not cut themselves off from their families.' But she also cites the lack of timetabling and the total lack of advance planning as inefficient.

Walley's counterpart in Stoke's twin city of Erlangen gets the equivalent of a fixture list at the start of the year. She can see the whole calendar before her, she can see which days she will be in the parliament and which days she will be in her constituency and plan her commitments accordingly. British MPs, on the other hand, cannot even plan from one week to the next. 'I can't tell you the number of requests that I get for meetings,' says Walley. 'For example, you'd love to be there to hand out the prizes on a school speech day, but you can't tell them till the Thursday of the week before whether or not you'll be free to do it, because of how the vote turns out . . .'

Clearly men have put up with this confusion, and the new women who call for change are apt to be regarded askance. But Walley is far from wet behind the ears. 'I've been there ten years and I see every reason for doing things differently. If we are going to be a government for the twenty-first century, we need to do things efficiently and make the best use of our time, and that means a complete rethink.'

New Member Eleanor Laing, herself well versed in the ways of Westminster, having worked for many years as a special adviser to Conservative Minister John MacGregor, said that planning and strategic use of time were the key tools for the opposition, and indeed, all backbenchers. 'If you take that freedom away from backbenchers, then you do not get proper scrutiny of the work of the government – it gives the government too much power, and the parliament not enough.'

Gwyneth Dunwoody agreed. Timetabled legislation meant handing 'the government of the day – and it happens to be my government at the moment, but it might not be – a marvellous weapon'. Timetabling utterly diminished the power of the backbenchers to scrutinise or hold up legislation. But throwing a spanner in the works no longer stops the machinery. The executive's control of procedures is already so tight that this weapon can really only be used against other backbenchers. It is extremely difficult these days to inconvenience the legislative programme and impossible to stop it in its tracks.

Ann Winterton is fearful for the future of Westminster because of the mood for change sweeping through it. 'Many of the traditions that take place have a hidden meaning. It's hidden in our history but it's very valid. We do things for a purpose and I would be very sad if all that was swept away.' She is no enemy of progress, 'Of course we should use new technology', but change for the sake of change has, she says, inflicted serious damage on democracy: 'I believe that all the changes which have been introduced in the last parliament, really since the war, all have damaged the traditional role of the backbench Member of Parliament in trying to keep the executive to account.'

Many new Members were shocked, and some upset by the way the Commons voted. Every night at ten, and depending how many votes are needed, sometimes for an hour or two afterwards, Members are asked to file past tellers at desks in locked lobbies and record their votes.

Jackie Ballard: 'So far there's been over four hundred, five hundred people squashed in a very narrow corridor for twenty minutes, half an hour breathing on top of each other. And the idea that this is a good opportunity to lobby Ministers is rubbish. You're like sardines. The sooner we have a sensible electronic voting system the better.'

Jenny Jones similarly thought the whole affair 'worse than the Tube' and denied the supposed possibilities of lobbying.

'There's no way you could have a sensible conversation with a Minister.'

Jane Griffiths: 'The way we actually vote, going through the lobbies, takes such a long time. It's uncomfortable, it's hot and sweaty. I'm quite fit but not everyone is and you are shuffling along slowly for half an hour at a time and your ankles can swell up. I don't see why it should be like that, and I believe in voting in person. I don't see why you shouldn't have swipe cards or something like that, or buttons in the chamber which you could press, like they have in other countries.'

Linda Gilroy was in favour of electronic voting, but admitted that the old style has its advantages. 'It is a great opportunity to meet the Ministers to talk with them. We had a big millennium bid rejected in Plymouth which was very important in the city . . . and to be able to see Chris Smith, not just once during the week but twice, and arrange to have a meeting and talk it through was really helpful in getting things moving much faster than would have been possible if I had had to do it by correspondence or attempting to find him somewhere else. So I'd still like the lobby to go on for some of the time, but if there were three votes it should be possible to do it in one action, rather than repetitively walk round in a circle for an hour.'

Llin Golding was a vehement enemy of electronic voting. 'They'll lose their cards. In this place you get tired, you get confused. You need to be in the lobby so that you can meet people and lobby Ministers. You can always go there and say – I've written to your office three weeks ago and I have had no reply. If all they have got is a switch card, they'll be out of the lobby in next to no time.'

Anne McGuire: 'There's a certain satisfaction in voting. I'm a wee bit old-fashioned – I quite like the physical point of voting, because I think that's part of the job. It's also a performance indicator. You are here to vote through the programme you stood for as a Member of Parliament.'

Angela Smith thought they would cope with the problem better in her local supermarket. 'If this was Tesco's they'd open another checkout.'

Ruth Kelly: 'An MP's life could be transformed relatively simply by a different voting system. At the moment MPs are asked to stay on the premises for hours. Every week I get a whip and it says I have to be there every night at nine o'clock until ten, eleven, twelve, one o'clock and I think it's absurd. It's purely a question of being voting fodder and walking through the correct lobby at the right time.'

The government, in a desperate attempt to stem complaints, added another desk in both lobbies and cut the queues by a third, but complaints continue.

On the modernisation committee progress is very slow. The Whips are terrified that any electronic system with swipe cards and pin numbers would allow one Member to vote on behalf of colleagues lurking in their offices. A suggestion that voting should be allowed from the beginning of the debate at three-thirty and continue throughout the evening, also found scant support. Party managers said Members would vote early and go home without listening to the arguments, but of course few people listen anyway. They work in their offices, or hang around in the restaurants and bars.

The timetable, or lack of timetable, was a key problem area for many of the new women, who were used to planning busy lives well in advance, and wanted to strike the proper balance between time in the House and time in their constituencies.

Theresa May: 'I think one of the hardest things to adjust to as a new Member is the uncertainty of business. MPs have a terribly bad reputation for not turning up to events and that's partly because of the uncertainty of the House. Two months in advance, you say you are going to meet someone on a certain date and time, and then a week before you discover you have to be here for a vote. That changes your whole diary.'

In a surprising admission, the Speaker revealed that she was also sympathetic to calls for a degree of timetabling, which she agreed was a problem 'particularly for the women Members who've got families and things to do as well as lead a very big professional and political life.

'I'd like to know the programme for the year – when we finish at Easter, when we come back, when we finish in the summer, when we come back – this sort of thing. It is very difficult to do. There's bound to be slippage because the government may not always be able to get its legislation through when it wants, but I think we could have some sort of skeleton framework giving an indication, so that we might make other arrangements for things that have to be done. I went on an official visit to Australia last summer and I was able to do it at a time which was convenient to me and convenient to Australia because they sent me their whole year's timetable in advance. I knew when they were sitting and I knew when they were in recess and I could fit in with it all. It was tremendously helpful and it may well be here. I do put the caveat in, of course, that I understand about slippage and I understand about the government not getting its business through, but it's nice to have some indication.'

Melanie Johnson also wanted to see more precise timetabling. Limits on the length of debates would do away with 'this business where the opposition is actually effectively in control of how long it takes to get through an item. The Speaker probably ought to be in control and it ought to be managed to a timetable, starting earlier in the day and finishing at a sensible time in the early evening.'

Gisela Stuart favoured more rationalisation. 'A lot of what people enjoy – rubbing shoulders in the tea room and plotting and what have you – is much more of an ego thing, and I hope that by and large the women try to place their ego somewhere else.'

Jackie Ballard, the Liberal Democrat spokesperson on women, whose West Country constituency is at least five hours' travelling time from Westminster, ran into problems recently. Business was concluded by half-past seven on the Thursday evening. Jackie, like many MPs with far-flung seats, expecting it to finish later, had made arrangements to return to the constituency the next day. 'If you'd known you were going to finish, you could have got the earlier train home. It really disrupts your life and makes it difficult to make plans.'

None of the MPs we spoke to were in pursuit of the easy option. All of them were driven by a desire to manage their time more effectively. Jackie Ballard, in common with many others, did not take issue with the number of hours she was required to work. 'I prefer to work three or four days a week till late at night and then have one or two days in the constituency.'

Old hand Margaret Beckett, President of the Board of Trade, said MPs are like people with two professions. 'When you are not in the House of Commons or your Department or whatever, your constituents feel that you are free for them. Politics is always going to be a way of life, and it is always going to be one that makes greater demands on you than those made by the professions because every MP is in the public domain.'

For many Labour Members, the 'constituency week' system which Gwyneth Dunwoody and Austin Mitchell decried, could be helpful. The Chief Whip Nick Brown wrote to his backbenchers on 20 October, 'Following the successful trial of the Constituency Week system before the summer recess, I have decided to continue the scheme. As before, each backbench member will be allocated one week away from the House to work in their constituency. I am happy to inform you that you have been allocated the week beginning . . .'

A few of the new Members were concerned about the quality of legislation passed by the Commons. Judy Mallaber wanted pre-legislative hearings. 'Things like the Child Support Act. I cannot believe how many cases in my constituency relate to the Child Support Agency. Not necessarily the principle, but the cack-handed way it has been carried out.' Jacqui Smith agreed. 'You have to open up the way for outside organisations to have an input in the discussions and the processing of legislation. Perhaps at a sort of pre-legislative hearing, you ought to be able to involve other people. Allow them to come in and give presentations on what's actually happening with a Bill.'

But the Chamber itself and the way people behaved in it caused the most discussion amongst female Members.

Julie Morgan: 'You never know when you'll be able to speak, and you have to sit for hours and hours waiting. You go in and you are supposed to bow to the Speaker. I really dislike doing that, and find it an odd thing to do. Very peculiar to bow to people as you go into a room. And then, when you leave, you are supposed to leave in a certain way. It's all these sorts of things that I feel are very difficult to live with.'

Ray Michie: 'I would go as far as to change the shape of the Chamber. As Liberal Democrats we have always wanted to have a horseshoe-type chamber instead of this confrontational business.

'I didn't come here to be one of the glory boys. They love the power, they love being here. My aim was – much as I respect the place, and I think it's a tremendous institution – to take power away from here and back to Scotland.

'One of the best debates I ever attended was when the famous Edwina Currie was a Health Minister, and we had a debate on women's health. There were men in the Chamber, but there were quite a few women. There was no point-scoring, no political stuff and in the end we were agreeing on most of the suggestions that were being made – it was really just a question of whether the resources would be there to implement them. There was much agreement across the floor. No nastiness. It made a great impression on me.'

Nastiness and point-scoring are usually suspended for the duration of a new Member's first speech. As if to repay the courtesy, maiden speeches are supposed to be similarly polite. Even so, stomachs knot and palms sweat as new MPs sit nervously waiting their turn. The Speaker still remembers the day she gave her maiden speech: 'I was terribly nervous. I remember that lunchtime – of course, I didn't want anything to eat, I didn't want to be in the House. I went to the house of a friend close by and just lay down in her spare room shaking. It's very daunting to get up for the first time, everybody quiet and listening to you – frightening.'

Hazel Blears waited in the Chamber for six and a half hours. 'I didn't go to the toilet, I didn't have anything to eat or drink – by the time I actually made it I was just so relieved to have been called! But it was quite nice because it was the day that Michael Howard and Ann Widdecombe were having their famous spat so the Chamber was perhaps more full than it would have been for a normal maiden speech. That was quite good, and I thoroughly enjoyed it. I was less nervous than I thought – but maybe that was the lapse of time.'

The first time Caroline Flint tried to make her maiden speech she wasn't called. 'I put my name down, and sat there for four or five hours, but it wasn't going to happen, there were just too many people in. So I put down my name again and asked the Deputy Speaker if I was likely to be taken and he said, "Well actually, you're on next." And so I had to sort of rush back to my seat. Another MP advised me to make sure I was plonked in front of a microphone, so my voice would carry. I mean, everyone is very helpful with tips and things like this.'

With 260 maiden speeches to fit in after May 1997, it seemed inevitable that some new Members would have a long time to wait. Others followed the Speaker's advice and deliberately put off making their speeches for as long as possible.

Betty Boothroyd: 'I didn't make my maiden speech for a wee while. I was always very worried about getting it over and I had a lot of advice: take your time, they said, it'll come, it'll come, and I think that's right. Get the feel of the place first, get a little confidence about things, find your way around, and then say what you have to say.'

The first time Jane Griffiths spoke in the Chamber it was to ask a question. 'In the middle of it there started to be this mocking laughter from the opposite benches, which I hadn't quite expected. I'd been told, "Oh, don't worry if they give any trouble Madam Speaker will look after you, she won't allow it." Er, but she didn't, she looked at me for a long moment – I think to see what I could do and if I could handle it. So I thought, well, I have to handle this, so I just spoke louder and drowned them out and carried on and that was fine. I think that if I'd totally floundered and not been able to cope with it she would have stepped in and shut them up. But she took that long moment to make her mind up whether I could deal with it or not. I respected that.'

The Speaker confirmed that Jane Griffiths had guessed

right. 'Absolutely. I mean, I do understand the butterflies in the stomach you get in a maiden speech, and I can well understand that they're standing there shaking and if there's any noise or any interruption then they can be thrown. I tend to sit at the edge of my seat and look at them intently, willing them to go on, you know, go on, you'll make it.'

Rather than picking on the new women Members, as a piece in the *Sunday Times* reported, she told me she feels for them very much. 'When they are standing putting a question, particularly a question because in Question Time it has to be a question it hasn't to be a statement, I can see the House losing patience with them. I don't want them to be barracked by the House and therefore sometimes I call them to order or say, "I think it's time now that you moved into a question not just a statement," and if I do that I do it meaning to be helpful because I want to protect them from any barracking that may come from colleagues who are losing patience.

'I'm something between a schoolmistress and a nanny in this job. Sometimes I do think, is that my voice? Am I so tough? Perhaps I ought to temper myself a little more. I have to stand back and think of that. Am I a bit hard, am I too abrasive? Sometimes I think I'm a little too soft you know, on occasions when I am more tolerant perhaps than I should be. But it's all in life's rich pattern here.

'It was splendid to see so many women coming into this House. I looked up in to the galleries and I thought there are the old suffragettes up there looking down as if saying, well girls you've not done too badly, you know, try a little harder get more . . . But it was great to see so many women here. I had enormous difficulties with the names of hundreds of new Members and I still have tremendous difficulties. The women are very helpful because, if I may say so, they're rather more colourful!'

How women behave in the Chamber, the fact that they express themselves in a different way and take little pleasure in shouting, has been much discussed at Westminster since 1 May. According to the Speaker, 'They are not as robust, if I may put it in those terms, as men are. They show great signs of emotion and passion, but they are not sitting there shouting, interrupting from a sedentary position like many of the men are.'

Patricia Hewitt: 'I don't shout. You just sit there saying, not very quietly, how revolting they are. We were doing a certain amount of that this afternoon. One of the Whips said there wasn't enough noise and enough support and cheering coming over.'

Janet Anderson is a government Whip, and said that, in her early days she was much put off by the aggressiveness of the Chamber, what she called the 'ya boo approach'. But after a while, she saw its logic. 'You begin to realise that there's a good reason for it. It's to put the other side off.' And now it's Janet's job to encourage the 101 Labour women Members to be more aggressive and make more noise.

'They don't like doing it, but I'll tell you why it is important. We have to keep saying telling them – our Ministers are facing the opposition. When you are making a speech from the Dispatch Box, you're facing the opposition, and unless there's some kind of noise coming from behind you, you have got no way of knowing what the reaction of the other side is.'

Kali Mountford: 'I can't see myself shouting. I have muttered quite a bit. If I think someone's talking rank rubbish, I just get up and intervene and tell them. I don't shout it.

'There were very unpleasant comments to Yvette last night in the debate. "Isn't she a pretty girl!" "Isn't she a feisty young thing!" "Hasn't she got nice legs!"'

Caroline Spelman: 'I sit on my side looking across at the women opposite and I wonder what they are thinking about and I see the same polite embarrassment on their faces that I'm feeling, and I think that's quite interesting. What may happen is that women find a different way of expressing their approval or disapproval, but I doubt if we are going to resort to that sort of low growl that was common before.'

The Speaker has been impressed by the dignified approach of the new women Members. 'I think this has a very good influence on the House. I hope that they will go on approaching speeches and questions in this way: showing emotion, feeling great passion about their beliefs, articulating that and articulating it on their feet and not shouting and demanding as happens sometimes here.'

On 7 May, when the new parliament assembled to re-elect the Speaker, Labour's new women wanted to show their approval of their leader, so they did what comes naturally and clapped. (Clapping in the Chamber, as in church, is frowned upon.) People have been talking about it ever since.

Jacqui Smith admits the new women have had problems in showing their approval for the Prime Minister. 'Whereas the Tories are mostly male and are used to going *Waaaar! Waaar! Waaar!* most of us found that very alien, and we weren't able to do it. We've had discussion about how we can show we think what Tony is saying is right without sounding like a bunch of silly old buffers.'

Judy Mallaber agreed. 'As women we find it very hard to do the hear-hear stuff.'

Patricia Hewitt: 'There's a silly rule that you are not allowed to clap in the House. I think you need a bit of drama. In the wind-up the other day Estelle Morris had to do quite a difficult speech, we were cheering her on and there was a lot of very positive noise and applause. Estelle said she just felt so buoyed up by having all these people here, all these women, new women, cheering her on. She just sailed through her speech and swept the Tories aside, whereas if we had all been quiet, it's very depressing for the person who's speaking and it's taken as disagreement.'

Very few of the new women were prepared to admit that they enjoyed the Chamber the way it is now. Oona King said she didn't mind any verbal aggression really. 'I'm always telling myself – oh my God, be more mature, act like a woman instead of shouting back. The reason it's difficult for women to get selected is because they don't necessarily excel in that kind of verbal combat – because they are more sensible and talk things through.'

Claire Curtis-Thomas told me she loves being in the Chamber. 'People say things that almost cause me to collapse, actually, they're just breathtaking. I can't believe that people actually say these things to one another. I have grown up and worked in an environment where professional etiquette is all . . . only oblique references when you doubt somebody's character. But here there's none of that. It's totally overt.'

According to Maria Eagle, the Chamber is a 'bit of a bear pit' and a certain amount of bear-pit behaviour has therefore to be expected. Asked how she'd react if anyone dared to fling an insult across the Chamber floor at her, she was undaunted. 'I won't tell you what I'd probably say back. I think you expect it in a sense. When it gets really offensive, I think it can be shocking, but I wouldn't take it without responding in kind.'

Beverley Hughes, who was Leader of Trafford Borough Council, suggested that the men about the House, Deputy Speakers and people from the Serjeant-at-Arms' office were finding it difficult to get used to the new women. 'I often find, especially if we are in the Chamber with one of the Deputy Speakers, that women are less likely to be called. A number of people have raised it informally with the Whips because there was an incident last week in business questions – there were about four of us standing up and trying to ask questions and I think eventually we all got called, but we were the last. I'm not saying for a minute that the Deputy Speaker is sitting there and saying "I'm not going to call women." It's just the product of his perspective and the culture of the place.'

Beverley Hughes enlightened us about another rather more bizarre difficulty faced by the Westminster women – that of mistaken identity. 'I've got vaguely auburn hair and glasses,' she told us, 'and Karen Buck, Judy Mallaber and I keep getting mistaken for each other. The same is true for another group of women.' It is almost as if Westminster, so unused to having women in its corridors, regards them as all the same. A Deputy Speaker even went so far as to call Hughes 'Karen Buck' to her face. He then 'apologised profusely because he was mortified to have made a mistake'.

There is no doubt that the staff of the House will get used to having more women around, but whether the modernisation sought by most of the women will occur is another matter. Things move slowly at Westminster, even on the modernisation committee. It could take years to agree an update for the voting system, and the idea of a timetable that lets Members know in advance what they're going to be doing next month or next session is anathema to government and opposition alike, neither of whom want their hands tied.

Margaret Ewing: 'I've visited parliaments throughout Europe and I've been in the Baltic states. I've been in Russia and they're all much more modern and more organised.'

A member of the modernisation committee told me that progress is almost painfully slow. The Conservatives, traditionalists anyway, are keen to practise their role as official opposition. They oppose almost every suggestion for bringing things up to date. But even the senior Labour Party Members turn out to be great respecters of Westminster traditions. No one really wants to see the place turned into a modern working parliament overnight. Betty Boothroyd maintains that tradition has a place in the House: 'The tradition of the Speaker's procession, the mace, the State opening by the Queen. There are lots of traditions here which are absolutely right which I will fight to maintain. There are other things of course where we must bring us into line – technology, for example: we put our order paper on the Internet. One favours all that sort of progress, it's absolutely right.'

None of the dramatic changes proposed to us by many new Members – electronic voting, efficient timetabling to allow advance planning, and pre-legislative hearings with people outside Westminster – are seriously in prospect in this parliament. But in Madam Speaker the new women Members may have found a surprising ally for some of their requests. 'I always regard myself as Speaker as the servant of the House. I don't dictate what it does, they tell me what they want me to do.'

It's a demanding role, and one that depends on her absolute impartiality and integrity. Was she ever lonely, I wondered?

'Not at all. I've too much on my mind and too much to do to be lonely. Sometimes I wish I had more space. I don't know what it is to be lonely – I'm very lucky don't you think? You see, loneliness isn't just having lots of people around you and then you're not. You can be lonely and have lots of people around.

'There have been one or two occasions, not recently but perhaps in my first years as Speaker, when I had to make decisions . . . I go upstairs and I look out at the Thames through the window and I think, "Oh my goodness I hope I've made the right decision," and if you call that loneliness – it's not really loneliness – just worry, concern for a little while. I've always made the right decision thank goodness. I'm pleased about that. I've got confidence in myself to know that I do make the decisions and they are right ones, not always popular ones, but they're right ones. So that's the time you might feel a little bit lonely, because when the buck stops you can have all the marvellous advice you want – and the advice here is the *crème de la crème*, I get the best possible advice – but when the buck stops I have to make the decision and I hope I do it, I hope I will continue to do it correctly.'

II

YESTERDAY IN PARLIAMENT

IN 1917 A NEW political Party, the Women's Party, was founded from the radical wing of the suffragette movement. Although 'in no way based on sex antagonism', its manifesto stated that 'women can best save the nation by keeping clear of men's party political machinery and traditions which, by universal consent, leave so much to be desired'. Set up on a right-wing, patriotic basis, the Party was in fact a thin disguise for Christabel Pankhurst's personal ambition to become the first elected woman MP. She stood as its only candidate in the newly created Smethwick constituency in the general election of 1918. Although the results were so close run that there had to be a recount, she failed to win the seat and, soon afterwards, the Party was wound up due to lack of funds.

As a tactic, 'keeping clear of men's party political machinery and traditions' has been rejected by most politically minded women ever since. However flawed the institution of parliament has been, women have fought in increasing numbers for the honour and privilege of a job at Westminster.

In 1918, when Countess Markievicz won the constituency of Dublin St Patrick's for Sinn Fein, seventeen of the 1,623 parliamentary candidates were women: just a little over 1 per cent. By 1945, the proportion had risen to 4.9 per cent and in 1992, when there were 366 women candidates out of 2,003 in total, this had gone up to 18.3 per cent.

However hard they may have fought for their seats, women MPs have always been a minority in the House, and have always seen themselves that way. Right from the start, there has been on-going debate about how they should organise their political approach and exactly what policies that approach should include. Partly this is a debate about how, or whether, our oldest political institutions should be altered to incorporate women. For instance, should there be separate women's sections within the political Parties, a separate Women's Conference, and a Parliamentary Women's Committee? Or would these just reinforce the 'ghetto' that women in politics have been struggling to escape?

More significantly, it is an argument about issues. In the debate preceding the Parliament (Qualification of Women) Bill, Lord Robert Cecil argued that 'we should treat [women] as human beings with absolutely equal rights with men'. More importantly, it was seen as the only way to get the concerns of women addressed by a male-dominated government. If, as George Bernard Shaw wrote in 1945, 'men cannot be trusted to behave themselves properly in the absence of women where the interests of their better halves are concerned', then women would have to represent their interests themselves. Throughout the 1918 debate ran the assumption that women would bring something new and different to the House of Commons: an agenda of their own.

Some, like the Duchess of Atholl, Conservative Member for Perth and Kinross, elected in 1923, were opposed to the idea of a women's agenda. In the early years of her parliamentary career she consistently voted against 'women's issue' proposals, such as the 1924 attempt to lower the age at which women could vote to twenty-one – the famous 'Flapper Vote'.

But, in general, the principle that women politicians would have particular causes and interests of their own was widely accepted. At last, wrote Eleanor Rathbone in 1925, 'we can demand what we want for women, not because it is what men have got, but because it is what women need to fulfil the potentialities of their own natures and to adjust themselves to the circumstances of their own lives.'

Disagreements arose, however, when it came to defining exactly what those causes and interests should be. Different parties and generations had different ideas. In the 1920s and early 1930s, attention focused largely on measures for the protection of women and children. This period saw the passage of the government's Guardianship of Infants Bill, which was designed to give mothers legal rights over their children. The debate on Margaret Bondfield's private Bill of 1928, to provide shoes for poor children, was the first proposal to gain organised, unanimous support from the women in the House. These years also saw the Married Women's (Maintenance) Act, the Law of Property Act, and the Matrimonial Causes Act pass on to the statute book.

As tension grew on the Continent and war seemed increasingly likely, the women MPs showed growing concern about the question of peace. Moving the Address in reply to the Speech from the Throne in 1936, Florence Horsbrugh spoke of the need for proper defences, and an unexpected partnership was formed between the Duchess of Atholl, Eleanor Rathbone and Ellen Wilkinson following Mussolini's attack on Abyssinia and the outbreak of the Spanish Civil War.

Many of the twenty-four women returned to the House in the 1945 general election described themselves as 'housewives' and, not surprisingly, attention focused again on domestic concerns in the years of post-war rationing. In the 1950 general election, Margaret Herbison, Florence Horsbrugh and Megan Lloyd George were chosen by the Labour, Conservative and Liberal Parties respectively to broadcast manifesto promises in an attempt to exploit the assumption that 'Women who all have to manage homes and . . . bring up children are practical, know where the shoe pinches' to try and win votes. One of these, Jean Mann, was still calling for a Housewives' Union in 1962: 'The female counterpart of the Trade Union MP is still at home, and no one . . . seems to miss her from the House of Commons.'

The feminist MP, Dr Edith Summerskill, welcomed the creation of new Ministries of Health, Education, Food, National Insurance and Housing on the grounds that 'more and more women will be attracted to the world of politics and more and more people will recognise that they can make a valuable contribution in a sphere in which they find themselves very much "at home"'.

The idea that women MPs would somehow be more naturally 'at home' in family-based areas such as health and education seemed wrong to the generation that followed Dr Summerskill. Interviewed for this book, Barbara Castle told a revealing story about her first days on the St Pancras Borough Council. She was twenty-seven and a colleague recommended her for the maternity and child welfare committee. 'I said, "Look, I'm not married and I've no children. You are both. You go on the maternity and child welfare committee. I want to go on the Highway, Sewers and Public Works."'

Similarly, Margaret Beckett wished she hadn't been given the job of junior Education Minister, and on the eve of the 1979 general election she told Melanie Phillips, author of *The Divided House*, 'I've decided that if we win the next election and I'm offered either education or social services I shall refuse, because I don't want to become typecast.'

For the first years after 1918, there was a residue of sisterly solidarity. But with the election of the anti-feminist Duchess of Atholl and the first three Labour women MPs in 1923, any assumption that the women in parliament would work together was soon forgotten. Taken as a whole, women MPs seem to have shared roughly similar ideas about the kinds of policies and legislation they would like to see improving women's lives. But this agreement has only rarely risen above the traditional Party divisions. In 1919 Lady Nancy Astor, the first elected woman MP to take her seat in the House of Commons, sought to reassure the rest of the House on this very subject, promising that, 'We women disagree just as much as the men.' Ten years later, when she told the new intake of women MPs that she hoped they would 'function as a women's party', the idea was rejected out of hand. As Parliamentary Secretary in the Ministry of Health, Susan Lawrence was not above scoring political points against Astor in the Chamber. Right from the start women in politics were only too aware that the best way to win equality with men and create a role for themselves in parliament was to join the fray.

With hindsight, it seems obvious that this would be the most practical approach: working from within to change tradition is a technique well suited to Britain's natural conservatism as well as to the 'first past the post' electoral system. After decades of lobbying for the vote, the decision to allow women to stand for parliament as well may have seemed a foregone conclusion. A former opponent of women's suffrage admitted in the Commons debate, 'You have the camel; you ought not to strain at the gnat', and the motion was passed by 274 votes to 25. But in fact the arrival of Nancy Astor the following year was of revolutionary significance. As late as August 1917 lady visitors wishing to listen to House of Commons debates had been kept separate from the rest of the Chamber behind a grille. Now they were to be free, in theory at least, to roam about the 'best gentleman's club in London' at will. And not as guests but Members. It is important not to under-estimate the impact of such a change. Perhaps the sense of shock was summed up best by Winston Churchill, who commented: 'I find a woman's intrusion into the House of Commons as embarrassing as if she burst into my bathroom when I had nothing with which to defend myself, not even a sponge.' Nancy Astor famously observed of her early days: 'Men whom I had known for years would not speak to me if they passed me in the corridor.'

Even in the 1970s and 1980s, according to Audrey Wise, women could never be 'in the company of two other women MPs without some comment'. Her male colleagues, she said, 'always want to know what groups of women are talking about, and they always think it's them.' According to Teresa Gorman, male MPs, particularly in the Conservative Party 'are stuck in the 1930s . . . They can only cope with women as nannies, grannies and, er, girlfriends, putting it politely.' It's a difficulty she puts down to the 'very, very masculine atmosphere' of the House – 'where they don't have to adapt their own behaviour to accommodate women'. Betty Boothroyd, who came in in the mid-1970s, agreed: 'Oh, it was a masculine place, of course – there were fewer women. I can't remember how many there were, but they were the stars in those days, and it was very much a masculine place. You would walk along a corridor and see notices on doors saying Members Only and you'd have to be here for a while to realise it didn't mean Members it meant male Members.'

There was a revolution, then, but one which women MPs have been keen to play down. Safely ensconced within the Victorian Gothic walls of the Palace itself, women MPs were quick to identify themselves with the established political parties and their confrontational approach. According to Gwyneth Dunwoody: 'We didn't go round saying – I want special treatment because I am a woman'.

Asked how she had been promoted to Minister at a time when there had so far only been two women in the Cabinet ever and women had yet to establish the kinds of support networks that men have relied on for advancement for years, Barbara Castle replied, 'I always went for the political argument and I'd made a name for myself in the House.' And it seems no coincidence that the higher up in government women have climbed, the more they have tended to present themselves as 'one of the boys'. As Margaret Thatcher said on the eve of the 1979 general election: 'I did not get here by being stridently female.' Audrey Wise reported of Shirley Williams, appointed Secretary of State for Education and Science in 1976, 'The whole time that I was in parliament, I never remember seeing her talk to another woman.'

'A woman's Party', said Eleanor Rathbone, 'is never possible because of politics.' Party plays its part. As Elizabeth Vallance, in her study *Women in the House*, notes, 'Women are in politics as people and not mainly as women.' Except in extraordinary circumstances, they have been 'too interested in and too divided by politics to contemplate any kind of corporate unity', tending to 'dislike the suggestion that their femininity has any important bearing on their professional life'. So, when Maureen Colquhoun asked Joan Lestor whether she intended to stand in the 1976 Labour leadership campaign, the rather fierce response was 'Certainly not. I'm not a woman, I'm a politician.' Similarly Edwina Currie is on record as having announced, 'I am not a woman. I am a

Conservative.'

It is not surprising, then, that women MPs have been ambivalent about the extent to which feminism and femininity should affect their political lives. Some, like Joan Lestor, saw being a woman as a distinct advantage: 'There are lots of young men around, but if you are a woman and are reasonably articulate and can state your case, you are noticed and remembered much longer.' Others like Barbara Castle, who claims she always saw herself 'as an MP, not as a woman MP', disagree. 'I only got my start in parliament through positive discrimination,' she told me, referring to an incident in 1944 when women Party members in her local constituency 'revolted against making the tea and writing envelopes for the men' in the fortuitous circumstance that there was no man on the shortlist. 'You do need to give women a kick-start,' but once a woman was through the selection barrier, she was OK.

Elected to a parliament described by Prime Minister Stanley Baldwin's wife as 'a man's institution, evolved through centuries by men to deal with men's affairs in a man's way', many women MPs found they had to work twice as hard as their male colleagues. 'There's still the assumption that if you're a female, you must actually be better than your male equivalent,' says Gwyneth Dunwoody. During the wartime debates on woman-power, Nancy Astor drew on the examples of Margaret Bondfield and the Duchess of Atholl to illustrate her point that women of influence in government were never returned to power, while 'men fail time after time, and back they come to the front bench'.

Women fought for special rights as well as legal equality, risking criticism from the press that they were concentrating too much on women's issues. When Thelma Cazalet-Keir's equal-pay amendment to the Education Bill of 1944 defeated the government in division by one vote, the *Daily Telegraph* asked in a headline 'WOMEN MPS' OBSESSION: ARE THEY ABUSING THEIR POWER?' and published a series of angry letters on the subject.

But women MPs have also helped define the role of the modern constituency backbencher. In Willesden West in the

1930s, for example, Mavis Tate set up one of the first MP's surgeries, described by the *Daily Telegraph* as 'a combination of labour exchange, house agency and centre for pension and accident claims'. Of course they never managed to please everyone. When they concentrated on government and constituency matters, the newspapers complained that women MPs weren't busy enough. In 1932 the *News Chronicle* published an article titled 'WHAT ARE WOMEN MPS DOING?' Twenty or so years later, the same newspaper reported the first woman King's Counsel's disappointment with women in parliament: 'They come and go; but what do they do? They go after the little-worth things but they will not concentrate on the great main issues.'

As Melanie Phillips writes in *The Divided House*, women MPs were expected to make some original contribution to politics and were, at the same time, attacked for being different. Robert Bemays MP complained in an *Evening Standard* article in 1936 that although it 'has been for years a platform platitude that women, now they have achieved political power on a complete equality with men, would be able to exercise an immense healing influence upon national and racial animosities', the women MPs 'have contributed nothing to our deliberations'. Thirty years later Edward Heath admitted he would like to see more women in politics – 'so long as they are providing what women can and not just duplicating what men can do'.

Edith Summerskill once commented that parliament was 'in some respects too gallant to women and in others not chivalrous enough', a subtle distinction, but one which goes right to the heart of men's reactions to women in the House. After the initial shock which greeted the arrival of the first few women MPs, it becomes progressively more difficult to find examples of overt sexist comment or behaviour. As you would expect, there are one or two notorious exceptions. For instance, Leo Abse's belief that 'essentially many of our women politicians are aberrant women . . . They are endowed with high intelligence but are fated by constitution or upbringing never to attain a full creative femininity' springs to mind. But the

women MPs themselves have been quick to praise the wel-
coming approach of their male counterparts. According to
Audrey Wise, one of the 1974 intake, 'I was accepted, we
were all accepted as individual MPs and you could be interested in anything you wanted without people saying, "That's
a funny choice for a woman."' Stories of muttered abuse and
name-calling, both inside the Chamber and out of it, however,
abound. 'What I found most irritating was the patronage,'
says Barbara Castle; men 'were afraid of the rivalry of
women. They had to reduce the women to a context which
made them feel at ease.' According to a saying of Helene
Hayman's, 'They either pat you on the head or pat you on the
bottom.' Shirley Summerskill observed that, 'More people
spoke to me when I got my hair cut than had spoken to me in
ten years. Could you imagine doing that to a man? They only
care what you look like.'

Whatever the reason, colleagues and journalists alike made
it impossible for women MPs to keep their gender out of
politics. And so did constituents. In an article published in the
Spectator in March 1925 the Duchess of Atholl complained,
'The women of the country have a charming habit of thinking
that it is they who have sent you [to Parliament] and that you
are only responsible to them.' Almost forty years later Lena
Jeger elaborated on this theme in the *Guardian*, remembering
how 'many widows from all over the country used to write to
me (and still do) to say: "You're not my MP but I'm writing
to you because you are a woman and a widow yourself."' By
attending women's section meetings and choosing to focus on
a 'women's issues' agenda, she continued, 'we lumber our-
selves with two conferences, two jobs, two loads of responsibility'.

As the comments of Lena Jeger and the Duchess of Atholl
show, women MPs found themselves held responsible for a
'dual constituency': first, the geographical group of voters
whose interests they had been elected to represent at
Westminster, and, on top of that, the interests of all women,
everywhere. And here again they demonstrated a combination
of political pragmatism and profound ambivalence, as with,

for example, the Equal Pay (No. 2) Bill, moved by Barbara Castle in February 1970. In her speech at the time, she reminded the House of Thelma Cazalet-Keir's 'successful revolt against the government on the issue of sex-discrimination in teachers' pay' and vividly described how 'the great man himself, Winston Churchill, had to come down to the House the next day to make reimposition of sex discrimination a vote of confidence'. Years later she stressed a different point: 'I didn't work for equal pay as a feminist issue. It was one of sheer, simple justice.'

While some came to resist and resent the demands of this second responsibility, others welcomed it. Many, like Audrey Wise, were forced to acknowledge the importance of gender issues by the political circumstances of the day. When she first arrived in the House, she told me, she 'hadn't realised that there would be all these very "women's issues" coming up and that I would define myself as a woman MP'.

In fact, the 1974 parliament saw an almost unprecedented degree of female solidarity. In their opposition to James White's and William Benyon's attempts to limit the 1967 Abortion Act, the Labour women MPs came closer to operating as a single party than they had at any other time since the Second World War.

Partly this can be linked to the new, vocal feminism of the period, which saw a rapid growth in the number of women's pressure groups. But the 27 women elected to that parliament (brought up to 28 by the Thurrock by-election in July 1976) were a formidable group in their own right. Twenty-three years later, 3 are still backbench MPs, 2 are Cabinet Ministers and 1 the Speaker of the House. The 5 women on the committee appointed to examine the Sex Discrimination Bill in April 1975, International Women's Year, fought 'clause by clause, section by section' for amendments as recommended by the Women's Rights Campaign and Women in Media, particularly to the language of the Bill, 'where "he" was used throughout to mean "she"'. According to Maureen Colquhoun, the men on the committee united cross-party, and 'consistently outvoted our amending resolutions' because 'sheep-like, they believed the government knew best and that the Labour women on the committee were time-wasting, time-consuming, and generally vexatious'.

The handling of the Sex Discrimination Bill demonstrated how women's voices could still be ignored, even as the government professed to listen. It also taught women to organise. When the women Members of the committee on the Abortion Amendment Bill resigned *en masse* in 1976, the decision did not surprise their female Labour Party colleagues: the move had been discussed well in advance. Audrey Wise remembers one sitting that started on a Tuesday morning and went right through, all day and all night, to Friday 'with just the Question Times omitted'. If necessary they would sit as a block in the House. When only two women were appointed to sit on the committee set up to look at battered wives and the women MPs complained and were ignored, they prevented the selection from going through by objecting, formally, every day until the committee was reappointed. The Whips' best strategy against this was to try and foster jealousy between the women, taking individuals aside to flatter them. 'We used to go back into the Lady Members' Room and talk this over and laugh like drains,' says Audrey Wise.

Predictably enough, they were heavily criticised by the press for sabotaging the Bill: as Elizabeth Vallance points out in *Women in the House* for using exactly the kind of bullying, manipulative strategies that men MPs use as a matter of course to 'get things done'.

The parliament of 1974 shows women from the same party organising in opposition to a single, highly controversial, issue. Significantly, the only time women MPs have been able to unite cross-party, on a wide range of issues was during the Second World War, when internal political hostilities were forgotten within a single coalition government.

In 1940 and 1941 women backbenchers and their representatives visited the Financial Secretary of the Treasury, the Foreign Secretary, and the Chancellor of the Exchequer to demand equality and a more responsible role for women in the war effort. A cross-party backbench women's committee was set up, chaired by Irene Ward, which met fortnightly while the House was in session, in Nancy Astor's house, throughout the war. In March 1941 the government was persuaded to allocate time for a debate on 'woman-power', in which backbenchers stood up and discussed the matters at issue 'like a well-rehearsed team' (Pamela Brookes, *Women at Westminster*).

This was one of those rare periods in the history of parliament when speeches from the floor of the House could bring about a change in policy. 'I am beginning to feel that the war is being prosecuted by both sexes and directed by one,' said Edith Summerskill shortly after the government had suggested setting up an all-male committee to investigate the welfare of the women's services in 1942. Thelma Cazalet-Keir asked pointedly whether 'it would be a good thing to set up an all-woman committee to enquire into conditions in the male services'. A new committee was subsequently announced comprising six women, including the Chair, and three men. The question of civilian compensation for war injuries was finally resolved in a division forced by Mavis Tate during the debate on the King's Speech in November 1942. Prior to this single women had received seven shillings less compensation than single men. Again, though, the argument was deliberately stripped of any 'feminist' connotations. 'I would impress upon the House that this is not a fight for women. It is a fight for human justice and nothing else.'

It was comparatively easy for women MPs to act together in the early years when their numbers were small and there was basic agreement on the need to legislate. Three of the four women MPs elected in 1924 voted in favour of the Contributory Pensions Bill in 1925, for example, and they all supported the Legitimacy Bill in 1926. Later, four out of six were in favour of the Aliens Bill in 1929. But as women like Margaret Bondfield, Florence Horsbrugh and Edith Summerskill were given government and Cabinet responsibilities, even this solidarity broke down. With the exception of the war years, when party political differences were suspended, it wasn't until the attacks on the 1967 Abortion Act in the mid-1970s, that any sense of co-operation between women MPs was restored. Judith Hart said she was aware that the Labour women MPs were monitoring issues from 1976 onwards. Even Conservative women, most of whom preferred to define themselves as individuals, on ideological grounds, admitted to Elizabeth Vallance that they were sometimes aware of an *esprit de corps*.

Seventy-nine years is a very long time indeed in politics, which makes it all the more remarkable to see the same issues debated again and again throughout the decades. Take the question of equal pay, for example. In 1920 Nancy Astor debated the motion, proposing equality of employment opportunity and pay for women and men within the Civil Service. Sixteen years later the Conservative government was defeated by eight votes in debate on the same subject. During a debate on the King's Speech in 1950, Irene Ward raised the subject again, warning the Labour government that 'women are very tired of promises without performance'. Four years later, after repeated questioning and a modest political protest (in which Irene Ward and Edith Summerskill drove from the Fawcett Society to Parliament in a horse-drawn carriage) the Chancellor of the Exchequer finally announced that equal pay in civil and local government services would be introduced, but it wasn't until the Act of 1970 that the concept of equal pay for all was turned into law. Injustices arising from the outdated idea that a married woman was the legal property of her husband also took decades to resolve.

Both Mavis Tate and Barbara Castle, speaking for separate generations and from opposite sides of the House, insisted that the issues of equal compensation and equal pay respectively be seen in terms of 'human justice and nothing else'. It is hard to determine what this shows us. Either they believed, along with Thelma Cazalet-Keir, that 'one of the tests of the civilisation of a country . . . is the position and status given to women' and were not frightened to give sex discrimination its proper name; or they knew, as pragmatic, successful politicians, that the House would not support the cause of sex equality unless the argument could be put in the widest, least controversial terms. It seems probable that the ambiguity was deliberate, a sort of camouflage.

Women MPs were defensive in other ways too. They worried that just one mistake by a female colleague could easily discredit them all. One senior trade unionist told me she wished Margaret Beckett hadn't put herself up for the leadership in 1993 because it wasn't good publicity for women MPs to be seen to fail. When the *Daily Mail* forced Maureen Colquhoun to come out in public as a lesbian, only one of her female colleagues, Millie Miller, spoke to her directly on the subject, asking, 'Now what are we going to do? We won't be able to have our hair short or wear trousers in public for fear of being labelled.' Audrey Wise moved out of the office she shared with Colquhoun, presumably in order to avoid being tainted by association.

I started this chapter by saying that women in parliament were always aware of themselves as a minority. No matter how hard they worked for their constituencies, how brilliantly they spoke in the Chamber, or how highly they were promoted, the demands of colleagues, the press and women voters made it impossible for them to keep gender-related issues separate from their professional lives. Some resented this, seeing it as a patronising, sexist attack on their status and achievements as individuals. Others welcomed it wholeheartedly, believing that, as women, they had an extra talent and responsibility to bring to politics and the fight against social and legal inequality.

EPILOGUE: THE CRITICAL FUTURE

1997 WILL BE remembered for ever as the election which produced a critical mass of women at Westminster. For the first time, women MPs are a group too big to be counted quickly. Too big for everyone to know everyone else. Too big to spot who is missing in a group photograph. But what happens next? Will the numbers go on increasing over the years, will they hover around 120, or will they slowly shrink?

Enthusiasts for positive discrimination argue that it should continue until gender balance is achieved. Clare Short, for one, is adamant: 'The truth is, political selections aren't pure democracy. It's such a tiny, funny in-group of people who recruit themselves into politics and put themselves forward to be politicians. To say that the existing mechanisms are sacred, and that any change will be somehow undemocratic is not true. We are not talking about kinds of selection systems that have the whole nation there as equals at the start of the race.

'My own view is that we have to be willing to change the law if we want to sustain this improvement in British democracy. Obviously it's not my area of policy now, so I suppose I ought to be careful. But I hope that that's what will be done.'

But it is unlikely that the Party will support her. The men at the top, including the Prime Minister Tony Blair, although pleased with the results of all-women shortlists, are not eager to repeat the experience. It will be hard for Labour to improve their score in the next decade.

The average age of the Labour Party in parliament

dropped from fifty-one to forty-eight at this election as a lot of older men retired, often shunted into the Lords. There will not be so many vacancies next time. And Labour won a landslide, so it would be remarkable if they didn't lose at least a few seats at the next election. These losses should be among the sixty-six seats which Labour had not expected to win, and where the all-women shortlist policy was not operational. Only eleven of the sixty-six were women, so in a diminished Labour Party after the next election the number of women could stay the same or go down a little, but rise, as a proportion, above the present 25 per cent of the parliamentary Party.

Before there is another Westminster election in 2001 or 2002, there will be elections to the European Parliament, the Scottish Parliament and the Welsh Assembly. All of these will include proportional representation as part of the voting system. For Scotland and Wales, the Labour Party and the Liberal Democrats are committed to gender balance, fifty-fifty, male and female candidates.

At their Party conference, the Liberal Democrats failed to gain the required two-thirds majority for some form of positive discrimination in Westminster elections, but they approved the idea of zipping (alternating male and female candidates on the list) for the European elections. The Party has consulted Cherie Booth QC to see if what they are proposing is legal. The Liberal Democrats want to avoid court cases. They would abandon the system if there was a chance that they could be taken to court, as the Labour Party was.

For the elections in Scotland and Wales, they are on stronger ground. At the Scottish Liberal Democrat conference when it was agreed to go for gender balance, Jim Wallace, the Scottish leader, wrote to Donald Dewar and asked him to exempt politics from the Sex Discrimination Act when writing the Scotland Bill.

It is to the main opposition Party, the Conservatives, that we should be looking for an improvement in the number of women in their ranks. The House of Commons looks uneven. A generous peppering of colour has transformed the government benches. The opposition benches remain resolutely dark-suited, interrupted only very rarely by the odd dash of royal blue, yellow or cerise. The Conservatives have only thirteen female MPs.

The Party seems to be still in shock from its huge defeat, and in total disarray. It needs new ideas to get back on a winning track, and I think it stands to gain most from some form of positive discrimination which would parachute women into winnable seats and change the face and feel of the Party to something more voter-friendly. But the omens are not good. Lord Parkinson has said he is particularly concerned to get more female candidates, but he looks uncomfortable and old-fashioned in his role as Party Chairman. And he carries the baggage of his poor treatment of a female prospective candidate for the 1982 Bermondsey by-election. Sara Keays, who had been offered the candidacy, found herself rejected when Central Office in the person of the Chairman, Lord (then Cecil) Parkinson intervened, saying that it would be much better to have a man as a candidate in a tough seat like Bermondsey, and that in any case he had 'better things' in mind for Miss Keays.

Lord Parkinson told me in October 1997 that attitudes had changed a good deal. 'What we are going to try to do is to attract on our candidates' list some very good women candidates, and encourage the Associations to make sure that about 25 per cent of the people on the shortlist are women. That's about as far as we can go.'

And as Labour proved conclusively over the years, that is simply not far enough. Nowhere in the world has a Party managed dramatically to increase the number of women candidates without some form of positive discrimination. According to Clare Short: 'The experience of most other countries in the world is that when one Party makes a breakthrough the public so like it, that the others run around and find a means of catching up. I predict that this will happen in Britain. It's just a question of how long it takes the Conservative Party. But I know there are mounting voices within it saying we've got to find a way of addressing this question, and it'll be very interesting to see how long it takes them.'

The Conservatives have always had good women candidates. Emma Nicholson said that by 1987, her 'High Fliers' scheme had encouraged 250 to 300 'classy' ladies from all walks of life to put themselves forward as parliamentary candidates: people of real achievement from a wide variety of backgrounds. Emma Nicholson said she believed that the Tories' greatest problem was that they just did not want women in positions of power in the Party. 'It's profoundly out of touch and out of date,' she complains. 'The new bedside manner of the Conservative Party doesn't extend to women, or if it does it's just as victims or handmaidens of the great men.'

Lord Parkinson says that it is a matter of getting local constituency parties to 'choose better' and Peta Buscombe, Vice Chair of the Party with special responsibility for women, says she thinks the most important message to broadcast is that Conservative women want to get into parliament for the right reasons. 'Any other way is an insult to them. We want to get there because of our competence, because we are the right candidate. I don't want to be, and none of my colleagues would ever want to be, seen as many of the Labour women MPs are now, as "quota women". This will always be a disadvantage to them.'

But Peta Buscombe is wrong. There is joy and pride in the ranks of the Labour Party, celebrating their 101 women MPs. Clare Short said knowingly that once all-women shortlists had been successful, it would be impossible to find a politician who had not supported them. How true that is. Ask any Labour man now and he'll grin sheepishly before he tells you how he 'wasn't sure in the beginning, but the results justified what happened'.

Gillian Shephard, expert politician that she is, smiles when I tell her what Lord Parkinson and Peta Buscombe are saying. She points out gently that William Hague has put her in charge of policies on women, and that the Conservatives are only really at the beginning of sorting out their recovery and their plans for the future. Gillian Shephard is the Conservative women's most valuable asset at the moment. Warm, funny, voter-friendly and sleaze-free, she alone among the leadership seems to understand that it is now up to the Tories to get more women to Westminster.

Teresa Gorman: 'I think the Labour Party women got their act together in the last parliament and they put pressure on their male colleagues. I think that was very effective politics. In politics you can do very little entirely on your own. You must have a coterie of people who will work with you on what you are trying to do. Now they've achieved a tremendous step forward with over 100 of them there in the Chamber. If they work together to achieve certain goals, and give women prominence and promote policies which relate to women, then the Conservative Party will see that a bunch of women can be effective politicians. So long as we don't do that, then the males in our Party will continue to disregard us or use us as a token face, just simply to take the sting out of the criticism. And that worries me.

'We have some very effective women . . . very few, but some very good-quality women, and if those perform strongly, and if we can put pressure on the new leadership to understand the significance of women in the front row, then we will have achieved something.'

For the 101 Labour women MPs, 1997 has been a triumphant year. Their Party has become the government, and they have doubled their representation at Westminster. There are 5 women Secretaries of State, the highest number ever in a British cabinet. There are 18 women Ministers and 78 women are members of House of Commons Select Committees, 9 of them on more than one.

Women in other political parties, and women voters now want even more from Labour women MPs. Everyone hopes that these women will do their jobs so well that they will banish for ever the reservations of men and women outside the Labour Party about choosing female candidates. Conservative women particularly want the Labour women to succeed, so that selection will be easier for them.

Like all political changes which move us towards democracy it seems so simple now. Votes for women in 1918, one in five women MPs at Westminster by 1997. Why ever did it take so long?

APPENDIX 1: THE FAWCETT SOCIETY REPORT

IN THE SUMMER of 1997, the Fawcett Society was commissioned by McDougall Craig Ltd to survey the women Members of the House of Commons. The following are some of its findings.

'A MALE INSTITUTION WITH SILLY RULES AND SECRET CONVENTIONS, MANAGED BY MEN, FOR MEN.'
Will the new women MPs change the culture of politics?

The 1st of May 1997 saw the highest-ever number of women MPs elected to the UK parliament. One hundred and twenty women were elected as MPs, 101 Labour, 13 Conservative, 3 Liberal Democrat, 2 SNP and the Speaker of the House, Betty Boothroyd. As the number of women MPs doubled from 63 before the election, the UK moved from 50th to 24th in the world league of women's representation in parliament.

The dramatic increase in the number of women MPs was welcomed as opening the way for a new style of politics. Campaigners to increase the proportion of women in parliament had long argued that once the number of women reached critical mass the nature and direction of political life would alter.

This is not to say that there is necessarily a distinct, female, approach to politics, that only women can articulate certain concerns and that these concerns are shared by all women. Rather, groups like Fawcett would argue, it would be surprising if the basic differences in men and women's life experiences did not lead to different perspectives on major issues.

While there were only a very few women MPs it would be very difficult for them to represent those different perspectives. A small group of women, facing hostility from many of the men, would have to prove themselves able to fit in with the existing political system. Any questioning of the style of politics could be seen as a sign that they were not able to cope. There might well be an assumption that women MPs would be naturally interested in the softer 'women's issues' rather than the harder 'real issues', so women who wanted to be taken seriously might deliberately choose to avoid 'women's issues' to show that they could handle real politics.

Once a sufficiently large number of women were elected, groups like Fawcett believed it would be easier for all women MPs to challenge these assumptions. A larger group of women could draw strength from each other to push for change in the culture of politics, not because they could not cope with the existing culture, but because they thought it was silly and unproductive. Women MPs could question the marginalisation of many 'women's issues', placing them at the centre of the political agenda.

It is too early to say whether these expectations will be satisfied. However, we can examine the attitudes of the women MPs for indications of their priorities and the way in which they might wish to work.

The Fawcett Survey of Women MPs

Fawcett, the leading organisation campaigning for equality between women and men, carried out a survey of women MPs between June and September 1997. Questionnaires were sent to all 120 women MPs and 78 responses were received, representing a response rate of 65 per cent.

Questionnaires were designed so that MPs could complete them themselves. Data was not weighted since the Party composition of those who completed the survey matched the true Party composition of women in the House of Commons to within 1 per cent, and the breakdown of those women elected to parliament before 1997 and those elected in 1997 was within 3 per cent.

	Number of Women MPs	Percentage of women respondent MPs	Percent of woman MPs	Number of respondents
Labour	101	84	65	83
Con	13	11	8	11
Other*	6	5	5	6
Pre 1997	48	40	29	37
1997	72	60	49	63

* Includes Speaker

There were 52 questions in the survey, covering educational, employment and political background, family responsibilities, the role of an MP, political ambition, attitudes to women's representation in parliament and strategies to increase it and attitudes to various policy issues. It is not possible to give a full breakdown and analysis of the survey in this chapter. I have therefore focused on women MPs' attitudes to women's representation in parliament and possible strategies to bring about equality. Responses to these questions highlight a strong belief in the need to change the culture of politics and the working practices of parliament among women MPs.

Role of a Woman MP

Labour women saw an important and specific role for themselves as women MPs. Ninety-five per cent of Labour women saw increasing the representation of women in parliament as a very or quite important aspect of their job. Eighty-six per cent saw representing women's interests as very or quite important. By contrast only 51 per cent of Conservative women saw increasing women's representation in parliament as very or quite important. No Conservative woman saw representing women's interests as very important and only 25 per cent saw it as quite important.

The new intake of women MPs first elected in 1997 were

more likely to see issues relating to women as important aspects of their job than women who had been elected before 1997. Ninety-four per cent of women first elected in 1997 believed that increasing the representation of women in parliament was very or quite important, compared to 86 per cent of women elected before 1997. Eighty-six per cent of the 1997 intake saw representing women's issues as very or quite important compared with 72 per cent of women elected before 1997.

Women's Representation in Parliament

Perhaps unsurprisingly, the majority (87 per cent) of women thought that it was very or fairly important to get women elected to parliament in equal numbers with men. The majority of the 10 per cent who thought that it was not very or not at all important were Conservative women. Thirty-eight per cent of Conservative women thought that it was not very important and 25 per cent thought that it was not at all important to have equal numbers of men and women elected to parliament.

Conservative and Labour women gave different explanations for the lack of women in parliament. All Conservative women agreed or agreed strongly with the statements, 'Women don't come forward to be considered', and 'Women put their families above becoming an MP', compared to 54 per cent of Labour women who thought that women did not come forward and 58 per cent who thought that women put their families before becoming an MP. Labour women were most likely to blame selection committees for not selecting women. Seventy-seven per cent of Labour women agreed or agreed strongly that 'Women are not given the opportunity by the parties' selection committees'. Sixty-three per cent of Conservative women agreed with this statement, although none agreed strongly.

Newly elected women were far more likely to blame selection committees than women elected before 1997: 88 per cent of women first elected in 1997 agreed or agreed strongly that 'women are not given the opportunity by the parties' selection committees', compared to only 48 per cent of women elected before 1997.

The majority of women MPs (63 per cent) thought that it was harder to be a woman in parliament, although a significant majority (28 per cent) felt that it made no difference. No woman thought that it was easier to be a woman than a man.

Respondents were asked why they thought it was harder to be a woman in parliament (or why it made no difference). This was an open question, but the same themes recurred in a number of answers. Fifteen women mentioned the problems of combining work with family life, two of whom complained that 'women do not have wives to look after them'. There were over thirty responses which focused on the male culture of politics such as 'male public school attitudes' or 'yob culture'. One woman wrote, 'the House of Commons is a male institution with silly rules, secret conventions (not written down anywhere or justifiable), managed by men, for men'.

Several women clearly found the atmosphere in parliament particularly unpleasant. One wrote, 'I have been desperately unhappy since being elected . . . I hate this place.' Others did not seem so unhappy but were clearly frustrated by what they saw as old fashioned and inefficient ways of working, writing 'time is used inefficiently, e.g. the voting methods', 'things are so badly organised'.

Of those who thought it made no difference whether an MP was a man or a woman most believed that it was equally hard for everyone. A few women felt that getting into parliament was harder for a woman, but once there, women were more visible, making it easier to make a mark. One woman wrote, 'I wish we would all stop whingeing about being female and get on with being Members of Parliament.'

Proposals for Increasing the Number of Women in Parliament

Proposals for increasing the number of women included Party training programmes for women, all-women shortlists, better childcare facilities in parliament, changing the parliamentary hours to nine to five, a three-day parliamentary week, financial support for women candidates, introducing a proportional voting system and no action, Party training programmes for women was the least controversial. Ninety- seven per cent of women MPs approved strongly or approved of Party training programmes compared to 1 per cent who disapproved. Childcare facilities was the next most popular idea with 77 per cent approving or approving strongly and only 14 per cent disapproving or disapproving strongly.

Conservative and Labour women had different attitudes to the proposals for increasing the number of women in parliament. With the exception of Party training programmes for women, the majority of Conservatives disapproved or disapproved strongly of the proposals. Among Labour women there was strong support for all-women shortlists with 40 per cent approving strongly and 45 per cent approving.

Women first elected in 1997 were more likely to approve of proposals to increase the proportion of women in parliament than those elected before 1997. Thirty-seven per cent of women first elected in 1997 approved strongly of all-women shortlists with another 47 per cent who approved, compared to 28 per cent and 24 per cent of women elected before 1997. Eighty-six per cent of the new intake approved or approved strongly of improved childcare facilities in parliament compared to 62 per cent of women elected before 1997.

Conclusion

There is a strong desire to change the culture of politics and practices of parliament among women MPs. This desire for change is strongest among Labour women MPs, and opposed by many Conservative women MPs. Among the Labour women, who form the vast majority of women MPs, the desire for change is strongest among the newly elected women. This may alter as the women become more accepting of existing structures and procedures. However, there are seventy-two newly elected women MPs, more than the total number of MPs in any previous parliament. If they are able to support and reinforce each other's desire for a different style of politics and commitment to working to make this happen, then we could see a major change in the culture of British politics.

APPENDIX 2: WOMEN MEMBERS INTERVIEWED FOR THIS BOOK

Labour

Diane Abbott	Hackney North and Stoke Newington
Janet Anderson	Rossendale and Darwen
Hilary Armstrong	North West Durham
Candy Atherton	Falmouth and Camborne
Charlotte Atkins	Staffordshire Moorlands
Margaret Beckett	Derby South
Anne Begg	Aberdeen South
Liz Blackman	Erewash
Hazel Blears	Salford
Helen Brinton	Peterborough
Karen Buck	Regent's Park and Kensington North
Christine Butler	Castle Point
Anne Campbell	Cambridge
Judith Church	Dagenham
Ann Clwyd	Cynon Valley
Jean Corston	Bristol East
Ann Cryer	Keighley
Claire Curtis-Thomas	Crosby
Valerie Davey	Bristol West
Julia Drown	South Swindon
Gwyneth Dunwoody	Crewe and Nantwich
Angela Eagle	Wallasey
Maria Eagle	Liverpool Garston
Louise Ellman	Liverpool Riverside

Lorna Fitzsimons	Rochdale
Caroline Flint	Don Valley
Barbara Follett	Stevenage
Maria Fyfe	Glasgow Maryhill
Linda Gilroy	Plymouth Sutton
Llin Golding	Newcastle under Lyme
Eileen Gordon	Romford
Jane Griffiths	Reading East
Harriet Harman	Camberwell and Peckham
Patricia Hewitt	Leicester West
Margaret Hodge	Barking
Beverley Hughes	Stretford and Urmston
Joan Humble	Blackpool North and Fleetwood
Glenda Jackson	Hampstead and Highgate
Helen Jackson	Sheffield Hillsborough
Melanie Johnson	Welwyn Hatfield
Jenny Jones	Wolverhampton South West
Lynne Jones	Birmingham Selly Oak
Tessa Jowell	Dulwich and West Norwood
Sally Keeble	Northampton North
Ann Keen	Brentford and Isleworth
Ruth Kelly	Bolton West
Oona King	Bethnal Green and Bow
Christine McCafferty	Calder Valley
Anne McGuire	Stirling
Shona McIsaac	Cleethorpes
Alice Mahon	Halifax
Judy Mallaber	Amber Valley
Gillian Merron	Lincoln
Laura Moffatt	Crawley
Julie Morgan	Cardiff North
Kali Mountford	Colne Valley
Mo Mowlam	Redcar
Diana Organ	Forest of Dean
Sandra Osborne	Ayr
Linda Perham	Ilford North
Bridget Prentice	Lewisham East

Joan Ruddock	Lewisham Deptford
Christine Russell	City of Chester
Clare Short	Birmingham Ladywood
Angela Smith	Basildon
Geraldine Smith	Morecambe and Lunesdale
Jacqui Smith	Redditch
Phyllis Starkey	Milton Keynes South West
Gisela Stuart	Birmingham Edgbaston
Ann Taylor	Dewsbury
Dari Taylor	Stockton South
Joan Walley	Stoke-on-Trent North
Claire Ward	Watford
Rosie Winterton	Doncaster Central
Audrey Wise	Preston

Conservative, Liberal Democrat, SNP, the Speaker

Jackie Ballard (LD)	Taunton
Betty Boothroyd (Speaker)	West Bromwich West
Virginia Bottomley (C)	South West Surrey
Roseanna Cunningham (SNP)	Perth
Margaret Ewing (SNP)	Moray
Cheryl Gillan (C)	Chesham and Amersham
Teresa Gorman (C)	Billericay
Julie Kirkbride (C)	Bromsgrove
Eleanor Laing (C)	Epping Forest
Theresa May	Maidenhead
Ray Michie (LD)	Argyll and Bute
Marion Roe (C)	Broxbourne
Gillian Shephard (C)	South West Norfolk
Caroline Spelman (C)	Meriden
Jenny Tonge (LD)	Richmond Park
Ann Widdecombe (C)	Maidstone and The Weald
Ann Winterton (C)	Congleton

BIBLIOGRAPHY

Pamela Brookes, *Women at Westminster* (Peter Davies, London, 1967).

Rachel Brooks, Angela Eagle and Clare Short, *Quotas Now: Women in the Labour Party*, Fabian Tracts, 541 (1990).

Maureen Colquhoun, *A Woman in the House* (Scan Books, Sussex, 1980).

Teresa Gorman with Heather Kirby, *The Bastards* (Pan, London, 1993).

Patricia Hewitt and Deborah Mattinson, *Women's Votes: The Key to Winning*, Fabian Research Series, 353 (1989).

Sara Keays, *A Question of Judgment* (Quintessential Press, Westminster, 1985).

Pippa Norris and Joni Lovenduski, *Political Recruitment: Gender, Race and Class in the British Parliament* (Cambridge University Press, 1995).

Parliamentary Affairs, vol. 49, no. 1 (January 1996).

Melanie Phillips, *The Divided House: Women at Westminster* (Sidgwick & Jackson, London, 1980).

Gillian Slovo, *Every Secret Thing*. (Little, Brown & Co, 1997).

Elizabeth Vallance, *Women in the House* (Athlone Press, London, 1979).